Canterbur

motivating your team

coaching for performance in schools

motivating your team

coaching for performance in schools

Peter R. Taylor

Paul Chapman
Publishing

© Peter R. Taylor 2007

First published 2007

 Paul Chapman Publishing
A SAGE Publications Company
1 Oliver's Yard
55 City Road
London EC1Y 1SP

SAGE Publications Inc.
2455 Teller Road
Thousand Oaks, California 91320

SAGE Publications India Pvt Ltd
B 1/I 1 Mohan Cooperative Industrial Area
Mathura Road
New Delhi 110 044

SAGE Publications Asia-Pacific Pte Ltd
33 Pekin Street #02-01
Far East Square
Singapore 048763

Library of Congress Control Number: 2006939347

British Library Cataloguing in Publication data

A catalogue record for this book is available from the British Library

ISBN 978-1-4129-2159-6
ISBN 978-1-4129-2160-2 (pbk)

Typeset by C&M Digitals (P) Ltd., Chennai, India
Printed in Great Britain by Athenaeum Press, Gateshead, Tyne & Wear
Printed on paper from sustainable resources

Contents

About the Author

Peter Taylor is an experienced and qualified coach, consultant, leader and board director; mainly in the field of education. He is qualified in Executive Coaching and Process Consultancy and Leadership (Post Graduate) from Manchester University. He is qualified as a Consultant Leader from the National College of School Leadership. He has an Advanced Diploma in Educational Management from the Open University and a Master's Degree in Education Management from Manchester Metropolitan University. Peter has a Bachelor of Arts Degree and a Teaching Certificate and he is a Fellow of the Royal Society of Arts and the Institute of Administrative Management. He has published and presented widely in England and abroad.

Peter runs a school that was described, by the Office for Standards in Education (Ofsted) as being 'outstanding … [with] a headteacher that leads with a very perceptive vision of educational innovation and reform, which is shared and celebrated by all staff and governors … he has the overwhelming support of the school community'. He works as a National Consultant Leader, supporting a variety of schools in their efforts to improve and/or sustain their success.

The National College of School Leadership, Manchester University and Manchester Metropolitan University employ Peter to work on their leadership, international and Master's Degree programmes. He also works as an Associate Adviser for his local education authority and as a Subject Matter Expert and Adviser to the Ministry of Education in the fields of performance management, quality assurance and data use. He is a Board Director and Council Member of the Institute of Administrative Management, the British Educational Leadership, Management and Administrative Society and Rowlinson Taylor Associates Limited. Peter is the British Representative to the European Forum for Educational Administration. He works as a consultant and trainer in schools all over England and abroad.

You want to improve your coaching and team leadership skills? You want to know how it can be that some leaders and coaches can transform teams and organisations?

If you look a little closer and listen a little harder you will notice that effective leaders and coaches don't change their teams!

Effective leaders and coaches create the conditions for their team members to change themselves; they motivate for performance.

Observe at deeper level still and you will notice that the best leaders and coaches are engaged in a process of personal change; this process never ends!

Foreword

Peter Taylor says that this book is 'written for busy people'. Well, we all think of ourselves as 'busy', but Peter truly lives up to the word. His interests are, to say the least, varied, and yet he manages to give each his full attention.

As headteacher of an 'outstanding' school (Ofsted, 2006) Peter has wrestled with the issue of motivation, and achieved results in both traditional and challenging environments. His own motivation has consistently been about values which 'fit' with the role. That is why he highlights 'strengths' in people because he believes the key to motivating them is to recognise what is important to them, *whatever their situation* (that is, their values).

As he puts is, 'An organisation must engage the hearts, minds and talents of its people'.

Peter tries to put this approach into practice in this book. There is a clear 'target audience' for each section, enabling individuals to pick out what is relevant to them. The case studies are qualified as discrete examples, but the argument is made that key points are not necessarily *fully specific* to the sector.

There is a tough edge to this work – which reflects Peter's own approach to managing performance – fair but firm, 'cool head, warm heart'. This approach relies heavily on truthful self-assessment and the plentiful analyses tools that help provide consistency to all the aspects of coaching he addresses. In this sense, he practices what he preaches – coaching relies on stability of environment and it is the coach's job to ensure each person changes with the environment, thus remaining stable – like a moving staircase. As a result the book offers an original and rigorous perspective with regard to many 'accepted' concepts and principles.

Perhaps most importantly the book provides an insight into the rationale and processes which underpin a successful experience for children in Worth School. Peter is nevertheless keen to point out that he believes these processes have wider application; the style and format of the book makes this a real possibility for readers – try the self-reviews if you do not believe me! I can only endorse Peter's message and urge you to take it seriously.

Ray Moorcroft

Acknowledgements

Thanks to Sheila, Charlotte and Emma for their support, patience and love. Thanks also to Brenda, Liz, Peter, Ray, Claire and the team at Worth for being great colleagues and putting up with my ideas and enthusiasms!

Introduction

This book is aimed at:

Busy leaders, managers, team leaders and coaches in any business or profession. The book will also be essential reading for anybody who has an interest in motivation, performance, coaching and leadership.

The book was written by a busy person for busy people; it is not designed to be academic in content but much of the content is based on sound theory.

Part I: Performance coaching

This first part of the book is designed to be informative and motivational for anybody who has a personal, professional or business interest in performance, coaching, motivation, management and leadership.

In these first four chapters I outline the thinking and motivation that underpins what I call 'performance coaching'. I suggest performance coaching is development of the recognised processes of appraisal and performance management. Performance coaching is designed to be motivational yet productive. The first four chapters can be read separately from each other or as one complete section. This first part can be read separately from Part II or in conjunction with Part II; Part I contains the thinking that underpins the practical information contained in Part II.

Part II: Theory into practice

This part of the book was written with the following people in mind:

- team leaders, business managers, senior leaders in any walk of life but especially education and other professions;

- senior leaders, middle managers, practice managers, team members, board members, directors and trustees in education and other professions; and
- those who have to implement performance management regulations in schools (including the 2006 regulations in England).

These chapters contain practical case studies drawn mainly from the field of education. In this part of the book I give practical advice on how to put theory into practice.

This book is about:

Helping you as a leader, manager and coach of people, to motivate and engage your people for performance. Busy leaders, managers and coaches will find this book is essential reading.

The style is designed to be accessible and useful with sections designed to 'lift and apply'. Checklists and practical guidance notes are provided to help you understand the principles and practice of effective motivation, coaching, performance motivation and management. I outline how these performance processes can be an essential lever in enhancing the performance and motivation of individuals and teams in your organisation. Examples, scenarios and case studies are drawn from coaching in several walks of life including sports, business and education.

Why is this important?

If you lead or coach a team of any size or you are a member of a team, you need to understand the basics of performance motivation, performance planning, monitoring and review. You also need to understand your role as performance coach and how to ensure your performance-coaching processes motivate and stay effective by the use of continuous improvement processes. If you want your team to be effective, to perform well and to be motivated, without it being damaging to those involved, then you need to know about sustainable continuous improvement processes and techniques. If you want to avoid the sort of revolutionary change that crashes into your organisation and your team, you need to read on. If you value evolution rather than the sort of change that comes as a shock and catches you and your team behind the game, causing stress and damage, then this is the book for you. If you like chaos and thrive on the adrenaline of shock treatment, then you really do need to read on and set about changing the way you operate!

Self-review

Before you read on, why not check the learning climate of your organisation as this is one of the key aspects of motivation? In terms of motivation and performance, is your organisation developed or does it have some development needs? Is your organisation open to learning, is it ready and able to change and adapt? If you complete this self-review now, it will help you assess the climate of your organisation as it currently stands. When you have read this book, undertake the self-review again and see if any of your responses have changed; I hope the book will have impacted positively in relation to your responses.

Measuring the learning climate in your organisation		
There is little encouragement to learn new skills and abilities.	1 2 3 4 5	People are encouraged to extend themselves and their knowledge.
People are secretive; information is hoarded.	1 2 3 4 5	People share their views and information.
People are ignored and then blamed when things go wrong.	1 2 3 4 5	People are recognised for good work and rewarded for learning.
People are not paid to think; their ideas are not valued.	1 2 3 4 5	Efforts are made to get people to share their ideas.
People do not help each other or share resources.	1 2 3 4 5	People are helpful, pleasure is taken in the success of others.
The higher you score, the more your organisation is likely to be a learning organisation.		

Now check your knowledge of the basics of the performance process as this is one of the key tools you can use in your drive to motivate your team for performance.

Performance coaching should be:	Yes/Partly/No
Integrated and inform training, development, target setting and development planning.	
A structured professional dialogue, based on objective progress/impact data, performance observations and appraisee self-review.	
Seen as being a key tool in helping teams focus on their core tasks.	
Transparent, rational, sustainable, low in bureaucracy and allows for unforeseen issues and problems that arise mid-year.	
Reviewed regularly by the users of the process with suggestions for improvement being accepted by senior staff, if feasible.	
Score: Yes = 2, Partly = 1, No = 0. **The fewer points scored out of 10, the more you need to update your knowledge of effective performance management.**	

How did you do? Read on!

Part I

Performance Coaching

Many of the limitations we have in relation to our performance are the ones we place on ourselves.

Coaching your team

This chapter is about:

Understanding the thinking of a performance coach. Team leaders need to go beyond the role of line manager, operating appraisal or performance management processes, as the best team leaders and managers are moving into the role of performance coach. Performance coaches seek to empower team members to be highly effective by reducing or removing limiting control mechanisms and maximising processes that motivate.

Why is this important?

Generally long-lasting and meaningful change in people is internally generated. If organisations are to allow their staff to 'shine', and make the most of their potential then the role of team leader as performance coach is vital. If an organisation is to become an adaptable learning organisation then it must engage the hearts, minds and talents of its people, and this is rarely, if ever, done by tight control. I would suggest that it is now almost impossible for any organisation with more than a few staff, to be effective by using command and control mechanisms. If the organisation employs well trained or educated staff, who are expected to make decisions or deal with clients in relation to complex transactions, then I would doubt a team leader who utilises command and control will ever have highly effective team members.

Appraisal and performance management processes have had their successes. Appraisal and performance management have enabled organisations to integrate their processes but some organisations have not yet seen the potential for coaching within these processes. For organisations to be highly successful their people have to be allowed to go beyond conformance and the basic requirements of performance management. Clearly, conformance to a manufacturing or professional

3

standard is vital in many organisations but for staff to be fully motivated and engaged they need to be allowed to rise above detailed control mechanisms. To foster this fully engaged mentality team leaders need to see themselves as not only managers, but also as leaders and performance coaches.

Self-review

How would you rate yourself in terms of being a team leader who can act as coach in an effective performance-coaching situation? Complete this self-review before reading the rest of this chapter and see where you stand now. At the end of the chapter you can repeat the self-review to assess any impact.

Performance coaching should be:	Yes/Partly/No
Seen as being a key tool in helping staff focus on their core tasks.	
The key to informing training, development, target setting and development planning.	
A structured professional dialogue based on a combination of objective data and appraisee self-review.	
A professional process that is rational, logical and conducted with respect.	
Transparent, with no hidden agendas; appraiser, appraisee and key senior staff being able to see essential documentation.	
Sustainable because it is low in bureaucracy; involving the minimum of paperwork.	
Flexible enough to allow for unforeseen issues and problems that arise mid-year.	
A process that is reviewed annually by the users of the process.	
Democratic enough so that suggestions for improvement are accepted by senior staff, following review.	
Score: Yes = 2, Partly = 1, No = 0. **1–6 you need to update your knowledge of effective performance coaching.** **7–12 you are getting there. 12 + the process is becoming effective.**	

So how did you do in relation to team leader as performance coach? If you need to develop your thinking in this area, read on.

Good practice

Team leaders, managers and senior staff need to understand and accept that one of their key roles is to coach their people, to help their people become effective in their task. Let us see how a leader can ensure performance coaching *does not* work – but in a world away from business and professional settings. This coach/manager is applying much of philosophy I hear when I work in many 'professional' settings, I hope you agree that this scenario illustrates the points of blockage in a 'tongue-in-cheek' fashion. The interviewee is talking to the local sports reporter:

Scenario: the manager

The board appointed me as head coach and manager of this team but I recognise my players as professionals. I don't watch them play, I stay in my office and supervise the game by marking and commenting on the written plans they submit before each game. Granted, asking such talented players to submit detailed written plans makes them tired; they spend hours producing the plans the day before the game but I think it is worth it as I then know what it is they intend to do. They tell me the paperwork demotivates them and stops them training but I think it is good practice to produce detailed plans. I must admit they tell me the game rarely goes exactly to plan but even so they do try to stick to the plan, even if the game is not going well. We have lost quite a lot of games recently and the players don't seem engaged, I don't understand why, our plans are good!

The players wouldn't appreciate my support and coaching before, during or after the game, I certainly don't want to talk with them about their performance, this would be unprofessional, its just not done is it? Of course the one thing we never discuss is results; in fact, we are not sure how we would measure results even if we wanted to. This is a question of philosophy you understand, we all have different views on this I guess. We judge how well we are doing by the quality of our play, not results; result can be too crude a measure. To discuss results may irritate the players and that is to be avoided at all costs. We are a caring club so we don't check results, we certainly don't ask if the spectators enjoy or benefit from the game, this would be too managerial. We value each individual too much to ask ourselves if a player is playing well.

(Continued)

(Continued)

In actual fact, if we have a problem it is usually not the fault of the leadership but most likely down to the players themselves, they can be just a little too individualistic and stubborn. I guess I will have to live with that fact as I am not sure what I can do about it. You see most problems in this club are the fault of the sport's governing body or the spectators. I wish they would leave us alone and let us get back to playing the game ...

How long would such a team manager last – in *any* area of business? Mind you I have been lucky enough, or is it unlucky enough, to be with several professional football teams when they have been 'briefed' by the coach and manager. The experience was a shock for me as I saw aggression from the manager and coach and a cynical detachment in the team members. I spoke to several of the team members after the session, on a one-to-one basis, and the players had no loyalty to the club. They had been switched off by the leadership. One well-known, household name, stated he could not wait to leave the team. The team dropped from the premiership very soon after, then the manager was replaced.

Leading organisations and leading teams are now incredibly complex tasks, not ones to be undertaken by well-meaning amateurs with no training in the task of being a professional coach or team leader. All team leaders and senior staff now need to develop a second set of professional skills knowledge and understanding, that of the professional leader. The time of the expert business or professional person putting themselves forward as 'gifted' amateur leaders is ready to be consigned to the waste bin of history! No matter how good a manager, engineer, teacher or lawyer you are you cannot trust to chance the leading of teams of expensive and well-trained staff; team leaders need to be trained and be professional leaders of men and women. We need expert performance coaches to lead our teams if we are to go from being average in performance to being excellent.

In contrast to the poor experience I have had when observing well-known football teams, I have spoken to and watched many top rugby players go from strength to strength when the management of the team has been professional and positive. The 2003 World Cup winning England rugby team being a good example of effective leadership and coaching improving further the individual talents of the squad. There are managers in football and American football who seem to take success with them wherever they work, and there are others that seem to breed discontent and unrest!

Getting started

As a team leader or senior leader, how do you ensure your people are motivated to be effective, are able to work within the vision, mission and plans of the organisation, yet at the same time recognise and work within some degree of accountability and rational control? This is a question many leaders ask themselves, and there is no easy answer, but every organisation needs to find the balance between empowerment and control that best meets the needs of their particular context, staff experience and professionalism. As ever there is rarely a 'one-size-fits-all' solution to this question.

Clarity and freedom to operate?

In my experience types of employee like a reasonable degree of clarity in their day-to-day work. Most recently I have been working as a consultant to several highly effective organisations and I asked them to identify what it was that had made them effective and what they thought would enable them to stay effective. A shared vision, philosophy and sense of direction was what most agreed gave them a sense of clarity and shared purpose. They also added other concepts such as shared or distributed leadership, suggesting the senior leaders 'go with the best logic' even if this best logic is offered by a person who may be a relatively junior member of the team. They also suggested leaders need to show trust, be open-minded and be informed by values they recognised.

It may not be easy but I have found it is worth spending some time agreeing what effective practice actually looks like. If your team can agree what 'good' is in your context, they will be some way towards creating their own, shared clarity. When the team or the organisation has agreed what good practice or effective working looks like, they would need to discuss how this can be evidenced, assessed or measured. In this way effective performance becomes an agreed concept. It is vital to test these concepts out with your internal and external clients/customers/stakeholders because if their version of good practice does not match yours, you may find yourself with a big problem. When you think you have agreed a rational and observable version of effective performance, you can then create a benchmark and quality measure to work within. In an ideal world this quality standard or benchmark would be internalised by your team, but in reality this limit of effective performance may be best illustrated as a set of parameters or limits that your team works within. If the parameters are not too tight and controlling, staff will be able to function with the maximum of freedom within the limits of effective practice demanded by your organisation in its context. I call this the 'earned autonomy model', and to date I have found it has worked well in all types of contexts where teamworking is essential but also where a good degree of autonomous

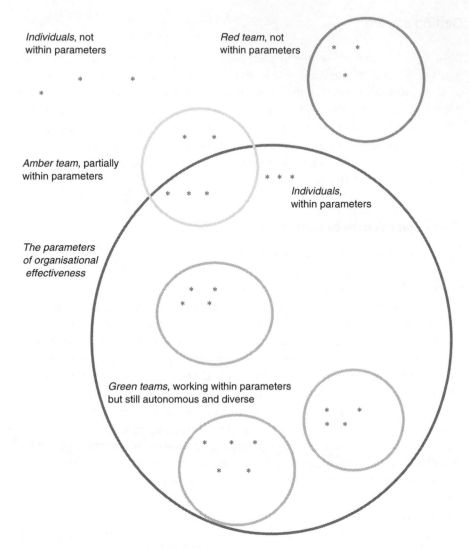

Individuals, not
within parameters

Red team, not
within parameters

Amber team, partially
within parameters

Individuals,
within parameters

The parameters
of organisational
effectiveness

Green teams, working within parameters
but still autonomous and diverse

Figure 1.1 *Autonomous and diverse teams working within agreed
organisational/business parameters*

decision-making and action is demanded of your team members. This model
seems to work particularly well in professional contexts or where staff have a
professional approach to their work.

Earned autonomy model

This model (Figure 1.1) requires quite a degree of thought but if you can hold
the two seemingly alternative positions of having clear and agreed controls
and maximum freedom to operate at the same time. In this way you can have

controls your team work within, you can ensure a degree of accountability and quality control, and have a sense of clarity. These factors seem to motivate as suggested earlier; people like a degree of clarity, and to have effective performance your team members need to know what effective performance looks like and know the limits of their freedom. You can also motivate your team by offering them a good degree of freedom to operate and make decisions; a degree of autonomy shows trust in the team leader and this again motivates team members.

This model is another form of effective delegation offering freedom within limits. Effective delegation is key in motivating your team and ensuring effectiveness of performance. This is where your coaching skills are tested to the full. You seek to ensure effective performance of each individual and team, but you now know tight controls do not seem to motivate or produce sustainable high standards of performance. As you become more experienced as a coach you will develop a 'continuum' of coaching, leading and consultancy style, all of which are correct to use in the right context at the right time. I have found the continuum of styles of coaching equally ineffective when used in the wrong way at the wrong time. There is as much theory linked to coaching, leadership and consultancy as there is to motivation, so I will not go into it here. However, I do include a list of works in the 'Further reading' list at the end of the chapter.

Coaching styles

Coaching styles can vary from the downright directive to the entirely client centred. In one mode the coach can offer clear advice, in another the coach may draw a solution from the team and in yet another the coach may allow the team or the individual complete ownership of the issue and the solution to that issue. In my professional context as a leader I have tried most forms of coaching when working with my team members. As a leader I found I could not allow my team complete autonomy in relation to their performance as we were all accountable for the performance results and, as such, I needed to have my say when the going got a little rough! This may be to do with my own stage of personal development but I think it is true to say most business and professional organisations are not democracies and it is irrational not to offer limits to freedom of action for your team. When working as an internal client-centred coach I could not let go of my obligation to the clients of the organisation where I am employed. I could not focus solely on the needs of my adult client (staff) at the expense of my main clients. I can easily work as an effective client-centred coach when working externally. When working with other organisations as a consultant I can step back from leadership and accept that the client owns the issue and the solution, as this is a legal and professional fact. I now adopt a more traditional coaching style when working with colleagues from my own team. I have accepted the ethical position that demands I put the needs of our clients ahead of those of the adults I coach and lead. In a more traditional coaching role I can accept that I have a vested interest in the development of the coachee and his/her effectiveness in the organisation and the team.

There are tensions involved in operating as a coach and I doubt an internal, full blown, client-centred consultancy/coaching approach can work to its best extent in one's own organisation with one's own team. Is the option 'to do nothing' real when working in the organisation that employs both the client and the consultant? In the organisation where I serve as leader I have a legal, professional and ethical responsibility to ensure effectiveness of the organisation for the benefit of my clients. Cleary, I had a vested interest in my team's development and I found it hard to 'step back' and observe success and failure in the way I can when acting as an external consultant.

Coaches and team leaders do not change people

When you first start to observe effective coaches and leaders you may wonder what they have that enables them to be so good at changing the performance and attitude of their teams. Even when some great coaches and leaders move from organisation to organisation, success, to a greater or lesser degree, seems to follow them! I have watched business leaders, headteachers and sports coaches, in a variety of sports, move from one organisation and take a degree of success with them. It would be easy to put this consistent success down to sheer luck, and of course a degree of good luck is invaluable in any business, sport or profession, but it is more than sheer good luck. If you observe closely you will notice that good leaders and coaches do not change their people; instead they create the right culture and climate for their people to grow and develop, to be at their best. Like an effective gardener they know they cannot make the flowers grow but they can buy good stock, plant well, tend the soil, add nutrients and protect the new shoots from extremes until they are strong enough to stand alone in the worst of conditions. The really effective coach knows how to create the conditions for good quality team members to thrive; in short they know how to motivate. Even the best coach, like the best gardener, will fail if the stock is of poor quality from the outset; to have a great team first you must ensure you recruit the right type of team member with not only the right skill set but the right mindset. You will get nowhere with team members who are determined to fail. Like an effective gardener, sometimes the conditions or the seasons are not right for planting, so as a coach you need to pick your time well. You have to have a good sense of timing, when to push your people, when to support and when to end a relationship or contract. This is not easy.

A really great coach or leader knows how to apply so many skills in the right way, to the right people and at the right time, but how do great coaches do this? I think really great coaches spend a lifetime changing themselves so they can be calm, confident, experienced and mature enough to reduce the background noise in their own minds enough to really see, hear, smell, taste, sense and feel emotionally what is actually going on and what is actually needed. This is a process of change that never ends for the greatest of coaches.

Be an expert single-tasker

You hear so much about 'multi-tasking' these days – this is the thing men cannot do well, we are told! When I think about best performance I usually observe people who are 'expert, single-taskers', not multi-taskers. There have been times when I have been playing rugby, cricket and squash where I have been 'in the zone' with a total focus on nothing else than the ball and the situation on the pitch/court. When I have been in the zone I have been focused on one task, I have given it my full attention with no thought of my concerns, my ego or myself. It may be the case that I have undertaken a series of single tasks very quickly but at no time was I doing two separate things at once, at least not in my conscious mind (clearly I was breathing and pumping blood, but not consciously at that moment).

In performance coaching, especially in one-to-one coaching or review meetings, single-tasking helps you really see, hear, smell, touch and sense with clarity of mind. If you single-task well, your full attention will be focused on the signals the individual in front of you is giving off, which in turn helps you understand what their issues and concerns may be even if they do not actually tell you what these are. As an effective single-tasker you can then start to help your team member explore issues they may not yet be fully conscious of. This level of awareness and skill takes sensitivity and experience but once the benefits of single-tasking are recognised you will not want to go back to multi-tasking. When it comes to coaching and working with your team members you need to focus on them, their performance, their concerns, their body language, mannerisms, tone of voice, eye movement, and so on. If you are undertaking a one-to-one coaching session or meeting, you need to put the team member at the centre of the meeting. You need to remove all other distractions such as phone calls, interruptions, excess heat or cold so you and your coachee can really plumb the depths of perception and feelings, not just talk of surface issues in between phone calls and interruptions. This is no easy task, especially for a busy manager or team leader surrounded by other people and ringing phones, but it needs to be done if your team member is to be valued, heard and motivated by the coaching session. So, should we start a light-hearted movement against the much credited multi-taskers and their "attention deficit" working methods?' Should we start a movement of expert serial single-taskers, hoping to bring some focus and quality back into interactions between people?

In performance coaching, as in traditional performance management, the annual review is a vital meeting. The appraisee is often a little nervous as he/she is going have all they have done in the last year analysed. The appraiser has to tread a fine line between listening, supporting and ensuring key targets are met and set. This is the meeting where single-tasking attention on the individual is essential. This scenario shows how not to do it.

Scenario

Jenny had had her appraisal meeting in her diary for some time now, she had reviewed her targets and other objectives, and she thought she had done well. Her team leader, Joan, had been positive in her feedback after lesson observations, and the mid-year progress review meeting went well. Joan had asked about training, development and progress towards targets and had assisted Jenny with a few minor issues. As a new member of the team, Jenny had been quite impressed with the attitude of her team leader and the performance processes in the organisation; in her last job it had felt like a bolt-on process and was negative. Jenny was a little nervous about the meeting with Joan but she had let Joan see copies of her draft assessments of targets hit and nearly hit so she felt she had done all she could.

At 9.30 a.m. Jenny turned up outside the room where she was to meet Joan. Jenny had had a nightmare of a drive into work and, to cap it all, when she arrived she found that the person who was to cover her tasks for that morning was ill and would not be coming in! Jenny had managed to get cover just in time for her meeting but her heart was still racing. When she knocked on the door Joan did not answer, in fact Joan was nowhere to be seen. Jenny sat down and waited. After a short while Joan arrived and stated that she was sorry for being late, she had realised that she had not put the meeting in her diary! Joan then announced that she had not read the draft review material, provided by Jenny, and asked Jenny if she could wait outside while she found the materials and reviewed them. Jenny reflected on life being less than perfect and left the room. After a few minutes another person knocked on Joan's door and went in, Jenny heard the two chatting and laughing for quite a time. When the person left Jenny expected Joan to appear and call her in, she was wrong. Now Jenny was confused, she liked and respected Joan but could not understand why Joan was so ready to waste her valuable time. After a little while longer Jenny started to think of all the work she had done for this meeting, in her own time. She also started to think of the work she had left with an unprepared colleague and what she would return to. If she could have known she would be sitting in the reception area for 20 minutes

(Continued)

she would have brought some work, but now she was stuck, waiting. Her emotions changed from being positive to being confused, frustrated and angry. It was now clear to Jenny that the meeting would be rushed and badly managed and that she would not be in a logical or professional state of mind.

Eventually Joan appeared, with a smile on her face, and asked Jenny to come through. Jenny managed to ask why she had been kept waiting so long, Joan replied, with a slight laugh, that the person who dropped in was somebody she had not seen for some time and that they chatted about their time training in Personnel Management. At that very second the phone rang and Joan picked up the call and started to deal with the caller. Joan called it 'multi-tasking' later, but Jenny was by now feeling ignored and undervalued. The meeting finally started and Jenny started to pull her thoughts together; at this point a knock on the door was answered by Joan! Jenny sensed an internal explosion of anger but she managed to keep it in. When Joan asked if Jenny would like to talk through the progress for that year Jenny replied that she would *not*, which was most out of character for Jenny. At this point Jenny got out her note pad and started to make detailed notes in preparation for her complaint if things went wrong in this process, which she now considered demeaning and unprofessional.

Later Joan was reflecting on the meeting with Jenny and wondered why Jenny was regarded so highly by all the other team leaders and senior staff. Joan reflected that maybe Jenny had had a bad day. Joan considered herself good with people and she had read all the books on emotional intelligence so she could not understand why Jenny was so detached and negative during the review meeting. Mind you, Joan had always thought performance management and performance coaching to be a bit managerial, and had never really found performance management or even performance coaching to be that useful. Joan wondered why so many of her colleagues valued performance processes so much!

A useful method

To ensure you at least start to allow your team members to create their own solution, to generate their own performance improvement techniques, there is a method of coaching that is well tried and tested. During my coaching and consultancy work, both internally and externally, the approach I adopt in most meetings is that of the 'skilled helper' as outlined by Egan (1998: 24):

Stage 1 Current scenario (What are the problems I should be working on?)
Stage 2 Preferred scenario (What do I need or want in place of what I have?)
Stage 3 Action strategies (What do I have to do to get what I need or want?)

I have found the three-stage approach outlined by Egan to be very effective. If you read more of Egan's work you will find that each of these three stages is subdivided but, in the heat of the moment during a dynamic coaching or consultancy session, I find the three stages sufficient. The meeting, be it an appraisal, review or coaching meeting, can easily be dealt with using these three stages. This approach engages the coachee in the process of issue and solution analysis, but the team leader can set the pace and agree, or not, the final action strategies. To be honest I find this three-stage approach useful in formal meetings and informal discussions. If a member of my team brings a problem to me, quite often I will follow the three stages and when the discussion is finished usually the team member has a solution and is motivated by the fact that I helped him/her develop it! This is also useful when dealing with team members who are good at 'upward delegation', which is another way of passing the problem to the team leader.

Scenario

Jill joined the organisation as a full-time secretary but now her life was changing, her family was growing and her situation at home could be regarded as 'comfortable'; she did not need to work anymore. Her family was growing and she wanted to spend more time with her children and grandchildren. At an appraisal meeting Jill was asked what her future plans and aspirations were. Jill indicated that she might consider leaving the job and give all her attention to her home and family. Her team leader, Jack, continued with the skilled helper, staged approach, to coaching. He asked what was on her mind. Jill told him of her thoughts, wishes and concerns. Jack pointed out that is was not necessary to jump to one solution until they had explored all the options. Jack asked Jill to outline what she would like from her role in school. He let her talk for some time and from time to time he asked a question to clarify a point or explore a little deeper. When Jill had explored her own thoughts Jack asked her what she thought the best solution would be, what would be an alternative strategy to the obvious one of resigning.

Jack and Jill discussed the options for action and agreed a way forward that would serve the needs of Jill and the needs of Jack and the organisation. Jill was offered reduced hours to ensure she could commit more to her family and enjoy the fruits of her hard work. Jill was also asked if

(Continued)

she would like to expand her role to further motivate her, as she was a very able woman who was tempted by a challenge. She was also very loyal and would seek to ensure her organisation was not let down.

Now Jill is the Business Manager, working part time. Jack gave Jill time to outline her problems and wishes; he then helped her devise a strategy to meet her own needs and those of the organisation A win-win situation.

From team member to professional

I have spent many years coaching my people in order to get them to a stage where they become self-generating, self-motivated and understand why things happen and what to do about them. I have found team members can be naturally effective but they do not always know why. When they hit a problem they do not have the depth of knowledge, reading or reflection to find their own solutions. These 'naturals' are not good at reflecting on, conceptualising or articulating their successes and failures. Action without an underpinning of thought, knowledge or learning can be unwise. Conversely, you may have team members who have 'paralysis by analysis'; such team members always need a bit longer to think. They can think of a thousand reasons not to act and they may be bound by theory and/or history. Learning without action can be unproductive. I try to get my team members to combine practice/action with learning/theory, as this combination should mean action is underpinned by theory and theory informs practice.

Practising	Professional action	Theorising
Unwise action: action without an underpinning of theory.	Informed action: action underpinned by theory and learning, learning that leads to considered action.	Unproductive inaction: theory without action.

This notion of encouraging your team members to think of themselves as professionals, not employees, is one of the key elements in the process of moving from performance management to performance coaching. Your team members need to be reflective, self-analytical, self-generating and be given a good degree of space in which to operate and make their own decisions within policy. Performance coaching will be much less effective if your team members are used to following orders as unthinking employees. You will have to work hard to move yourself and your team to the performance coaching mindset, a mindset that understands the links between motivation, respect, effectiveness, outcomes, success and performance in relation to the whole of the job or role.

Impact on your team?

The impact on your team of using these concepts and tools should be that they become more engaged in the performance processes and direction of your organisation. From personal experience of leading several organisations and working with others as a director or as a consultant, I find these concepts motivate performance more often than not. If you try one or more of the methods I suggest, observe the impact and then adjust the approach to suit you, your team and the context of your organisation. Make these concepts your own, or if need be, reject them, but I think you will find your team will be more motivated and effective if you move from line manager to team leader as performance coach.

Impact on you?

Now is the opportunity for you to assess the impact of this chapter on your thinking. Have a second go at the self-review and see if your mindset has changed.

Performance coaching should be:	Yes/Partly/No
Seen as being a key tool in helping staff focus on their core tasks.	
The key to informing professional development, target setting and development planning.	
A structured professional dialogue based on a combination of objective data and appraisee self-review.	
A professional process that is rational, logical and conducted with respect.	

(Continued)	
Transparent, with no hidden agendas; appraiser, appraisee and key senior staff being able to see essential documentation.	
Sustainable because it is low in bureaucracy; involving the minimum of paperwork.	
Flexible enough to allow for unforeseen issues and problems that arise mid-year.	
A process that is reviewed annually by the users of the process.	
Democratic enough so that suggestions for improvement are accepted by senior staff, following review.	
Score: Yes= 2, Partly= 1, No= 0. **1–6 you need to update your knowledge of effective performance coaching.** **7–12 you are getting there. 12+ the process is becoming effective.**	

If you want to explore further any of the concepts I outline, I offer some suggestions for further reading.

Further reading

Argyris, C. (1999) *On Organizational Learning*. 2nd edn. Oxford: Blackwell.

Block, P. (2000) *Flawless Consultancy; A Guide To Getting Your Expertise Used*. 2nd edn. San Francisco, CA: Jossey-Bass.

Boyatzis, R. (1999) 'Self-directed change and learning as a necessary meta-competency for success and effectiveness in the twenty-first century', in R. Sims and J. Veres (eds), *Keys to Employee Success in Coming Decades*. Westport, CT: Quorum Books.

Caldwell, B. and Spinks, J. (1992) *Leading the Self Managing School*. London: Falmer Press.

Cockman, P., Evans, B. and Reynolds, P. (1999) *Consulting for Real People*. Maidenhead: McGraw-Hill.

Collins, J. (2001) *From Good to Great*. London: Random House Business Books.

Egan, G. (1993) *Adding Value: A Systematic Guide to Business Driven Management and Leadership*. San Francisco, CA: Jossey-Bass.

Evans, R. (1998) *The Human Side of School Change*. San Francisco, CA: Jossey-Bass.

Garret, B. (1990) *Creating a Learning Organisation*. Hemel Hempstead: Director Books, Fitzwilliam.

Gold, A., Evans, J., Early, P., Halpin, D. and Collarbone, P. (2003) 'Principled principals?' *Educational Management and Administration*, 31(2): 127–38.

Hammer, M. and Champy, J. (1994) *Reengineering the Corporation*. London: Nicholas Brealey.

Heron, J. (1999) *The Complete Facilitator's Handbook*. London and New York: Kogan Page.

Johnson, J. (1998) *Who Moved My Cheese*? New York: G.P. Putnam's Sons.

Osterman, K. and Kottkamp, R. (1994) 'Rethinking professional development', in N. Bennett, R. Glatter and R. Levacic (eds), *Improving Educational Management*. London: Paul Chapman Publishing.

Parkin, M. (2001) *Coaching and Storytelling*. London: Kogan Page.

Rowan, J. and Taylor, P. (2002) 'Leading the autonomous school', in J. Heywood and P. Taylor (eds), *School Autonomy*, European Forum on Educational Administration, Bulletin 2.

Schein, E.H. (1999) *Process Consultation Revisited*. Reading, MA: Addison-Wesley.

Senge, P., Lucas, T. and Dutton, J. (2000) *Schools That Learn*. London: Nicholas Brealey.

Senge P. (1990) *The Fifth Discipline*. London: Nicholas Brealey.

Wellins, R., Byham, W. and Wilson, J. (1991) *Empowered Teams*. San Francisco, CA: Jossey-Bass.

Coaching for performance

This chapter is about:

Motivating your people to ensure success through the use of effective performance coaching. I use fictitious scenarios to illustrate how effective performance coaching can help you as team leader (middle manager, senior leader or director/governor) 'make a difference' for the adults and clients/students you work with. Performance coaching, designed and applied correctly by you as team leader, can be a key factor in the motivation of your colleagues and team members but only if you lead your team with good intent, integrity and professionalism.

Why is this important?

It is not enough to work from concepts, values and philosophies alone if you want to ensure performance and motivation for your team. You need rational, agreed, sustainable and effective processes to work to and from. The key process I suggest is performance coaching. Performance processes, if applied well, are motivating and liberating for your team members and ensure effective performance for the organisation. The concepts and suggestions I offer are designed to impact on your approach to the motivation of staff for effective performance. I will cover some ground relating to the concepts supporting performance and motivation and I hope I can offer ideas that can be 'lifted, adapted and applied' by you as you see fit, to be used in your organisation.

Self-review

Before you read on I would like you to assess you own attitude relating to performance coaching in general. Towards the end of the chapter I will ask you to undertake this self-review again and assess any changes in attitude. Please answer the following questions as honestly as possible.

Performance coaching should be:	Yes/Partly/No
Integrated and inform staff development, target setting and development/business planning.	
A structured professional dialogue based on objective information, data, work observation and appraisee self-review.	
Seen as being a key tool in helping your team focus on their core professional or business tasks.	
Transparent, rational, sustainable, low in bureaucracy and allows for unforeseen issues and problems that arise mid-year.	
Reviewed regularly by the users of the process with suggestions for improvement being accepted by senior staff, if feasible.	
Score: Yes = 2, Partly = 1, No = 0. **The fewer points scored out of 10, the more you need to update your knowledge of effective performance management.**	

So how did you perform? Are you already well informed about performance coaching or do you need to know more? If you did well, so far so good but if you need to learn more, I hope to outline the essentials of this key process for performance coaching and motivation a little more in this chapter.

Good practice

Structured professional dialogue

Performance coaching, like effective performance management, should be a structured, professional dialogue that reviews and enhances organisational effectiveness, employee motivation and professional development. It is a key tool in moving an organisation from being a series of processes, structures and separate groups of individuals to an effective, flexible and focused learning organisation. In the hands of leaders with vision, performance coaching can be transformational and enormously motivating.

Scenario

Graham joined the leadership team of an effective organisation. He moved from the South East to the North West of England to take up his new role as team leader and senior manager. In his previous post he had not been in favour of performance management and had not heard of performance coaching. Normally this would not have been a problem, however, the organisation he had just joined had used performance management, in one form or another, for many years, and had now developed an effective performance coaching philosophy and process. The organisation had been awarded Investor In People [IIP] several years before and was committed to linking effective continuing professional development to staff performance and client satisfaction and effective provision. Staff at all levels and roles were fully committed to the performance process at the school as they saw it as rational, based on output data, observation data, informing professional development and development/business planning. The organisation was so effective at using performance coaching and performance management, it was often used as an example of effective provision by local and national organisations.

Graham had not been at the organisation very long when he changed his mind about performance coaching. Being a professional who took his role seriously, he was intent on making a difference for his clients. Graham was initially sceptical about the performance processes, seeing them as yet another initiative that would add to his bureaucratic burden without helping him in his core task of ensuring effective provision for his clients. Within a year Graham was so positive about the performance processes he was now using, he felt able to speak on the effectiveness of the process at a national conference. Graham stated that the performance processes in this particular organisation helped him, 'make a difference for his clients in this context', and that, being an idealist, this is what he came into his profession for. Performance coaching was not seen as part of the problem by Graham, it was seen as part of the solution.

Transformation

So how did this transformation in attitude towards performance management take place? Quite simply, the performance management process in this particular organisation held coaching and development at its heart. This motivated and helped Graham in his new role as team leader and senior manager. So why does this process not motivate others who use it in different organisations? Well, in his new organisation Graham saw the process as a structured professional dialogue that helped him in his core task of helping his clients and his team members. In his previous experience he had seen the performance process as imposed and of little value in his core tasks. The process in his new organisation was not part of the problem but part of the solution. The performance process in his new organisation, was seen by Graham as intelligent, sustainable, not bureaucratic, and integrated with the other processes. It was not based solely on output data but focused mainly on progress/improvement (value-added) data and it took account of factors beyond his control. The performance processes helped him understand the best way to assist his clients and his team and offered coaching, support, strategies and resources, not blame. It was not top down, but professional and transparent. In short this was not the performance management process he had seen in the past but a performance-coaching process that worked. The performance-coaching process was valued by Graham because it was not a 'bolt-on' task but a key self-evaluation process. Performance coaching was designed to help staff improve their performance in a way that engaged and motivated them, whilst keeping a focus on output data and client satisfaction. It was a key process within a 'learning organisation' that was run by senior staff who were passionate about effective provision for clients and assisting all staff in that task.

Like many of the best people in most professions or businesses Graham is an intelligent, highly qualified, values-driven and independent-minded person who came into his profession to make a personal difference for the clients in his care. People such as Graham will argue that performance coaching in a professional context should not be about command and control but be flexible, intelligent and 'light touch'. It should be a process designed specifically to recognise a significant degree of professional autonomy, yet ensure and support effectiveness, teamworking and proper accountability for all staff at all levels and in whatever roles they perform. The performance-coaching process used at its best is not only effective at promoting performance and motivation but it can be transformational, helping your team grow as colleagues and people.

Use of data and objective information

For performance coaching to be effective and motivational it needs to hold the gathering and analysis of progress, performance information and work observation at its heart. Reflection on objective data forms the basis of good management information, which in turn forms the basis of knowledge relating to the organisation and the individuals, within it. This puts performance coaching and professional development on a sound foundation of data, information and knowledge. For those of you who are not inclined towards being evidence based in your work, ask yourself how can you as a team leader and coach discuss performance with your team if you do not have sound, relevant and recent information about their efforts, effectiveness and motivation? Well-respected and experienced team members are unlikely to be motivated to change unless you move away from opinion towards offering evidence that identifies behaviours and outcomes. If 'a journey of a thousand miles begins with a single step', then it seems logical and professional to ensure that first we know where we are and the first step is taken in the right direction, with an appropriate destination in mind! I offer more information about the use of data in subsequent chapters.

Getting started

Your motives as team leader

The first step that needs to be taken in ensuring effective performance coaching is to examine the motives, intentions and leadership qualities of those who are to lead and manage the coaching. If the leaders of the process are unclear as to why and how the process is to run, what chance is there of motivated but busy staff buying into it? If performance coaching is seen as a bolt-on process, or yet another task designed to take your team away from its core tasks, then it is destined to fail. All key team members need to be fully behind the process and understand its benefits and limitations. They need to understand their roles and be well versed in them.

The early days

In the beginning, your performance process will not be coherent and integrated but fragmented, having weak or no linkage between development planning, the appraisal/review meeting, target setting, data analysis, work observation and professional development/training. As the process becomes more effective it will hold the gathering and analysis of data, information and work observation at its heart. What happens next is that reflection on this objective information and data informs the appraisal interview, which in turn informs the professional development, coaching and support of individuals and teams. The cycle of planning, monitoring and review then informs the development plan. As the skills and capabilities of the leaders and managers in the organisation become more proficient, the process will move from being a once a year event to being the key process in understanding the organisation, co-ordinating and maximising the talents and aspirations of staff, and impacting powerfully on the organisation's climate, culture and results.

The process

My staff are fully committed to the performance-coaching process we use, it is rational, based on progress data, information and work observation all informing professional development/training and whole development planning. The process started modestly but, by a process of regular review and improvement, what Japanese managers call 'kaizen', manageable but regular improvement was suggested by staff and team leaders; the school prefers evolution to revolution. The involvement of staff in kaizen, relating to the performance management, has led to the growth and development of performance-coaching. It also needs to be said that kaizen led to the introduction of managed reflection, planning and preparation time to enable staff to do the tasks required to fully engage in the performance-coaching process. In order to focus on this process very few other meetings are held, there are no weekly staff meeting and virtually all professional development is organised within set training and development times. Ad hoc training and meetings are kept to a minimum.

Whatever performance-coaching process you adopt in your context, the key lies in generating an open/transparent process and climate in each phase of performance coaching. Whatever role you have you can influence the process in your organisation in order to ensure the best deal for the staff and clients you are responsible for. The process we use falls into three broad phases, as used in performance management.

First we undertake the audit phase. We gather and analyse a raft of specific management information and data. Some of the data is related to output or attainment data, some is related to progress or improvement data. We also use staff, client and society data to analyse opinion. We use feedback from staff quality circles and client quality circles (like a focus group). We observe work in progress as this provides a key opportunity to gather coaching information. The analysis of this hard and soft data and information tells us where we stand and what people think. Our data shows the effectiveness of individuals, teams and departments, and provides key information for coaching and improvement. We hold our staff review and appraisal meetings at the end of this phase. At that meeting we look back and review targets from the previous cycle. We discuss general issues and coach, and then agree future targets and coaching points. This meeting is open and positive; there is no blame, and coaching is the key process in helping staff review and set targets. The information gathered at the review meeting helps team leaders get an overview of staff need and opinion, this feeds through into training and development plans for individuals, teams and the organisation as a whole.

All the information and data gathered in the audit and analysis phase is then used to inform the planning phase – not only planning for staff coaching, development and training but development/business planning. Our plans are initially guided by senior staff but then discussed by the board and all staff at on open meeting, which we call the 'moot'. The moot is like a meeting of the team/tribe as in Anglo Saxon history. At this moot we all thrash out our direction and sign up to the future plans.

Clearly the next phase is that of implementation, when teams and team leaders get on with the job! We do review and set new operational plans during the year, as needed, but the overall strategic direction is usually kept to. This phase then links back to the audit phase.

So what do you think about the process we use? This process is recognisable as sensible management, it is the intentions, attitude and focus on coaching that makes our process tick. We find this process manageable, sustainable, motivating and effective, but you will need to adapt and improve our performance processes to ensure they are tailored to your context at this stage of your organisational development. I have observed processes in many organisations in many countries but to date I have not encountered many impressive examples of performance coaching or even performance management in other professions or businesses. Although I am sure very effective and motivational performance processes must exist, I do not know of any that seem to motivate and improve performance in as easy and sustainable manner as the one we use. So if your organisation has an effective and motivational performance coaching process, please do let me know.

Target and objective setting

You need to motivate your team by the effective use of target setting. As a team leader your team need to be effective in a business sense, you need output and progress/improvement data yet you do not want to overstretch your team members. You also do not want to 'under-stretch' them either. Overstretched team members become stressed and less effective; they burn out, withdraw or leave. Under-stretched team members get bored, restless or disruptive. So getting the balance right is key.

Now let us consider some detailed ways of agreeing and recording targets and objectives. Examples are:

- Specific;
- Measurable;
- Achievable;
- Realistic (Resourced); and
- Timed.

These are referred to as SMART targets, and are commonly used in target setting.

- Concrete;
- Realistic;
- Observable; and
- Worthwhile.

These are CROW targets that are used less often.

This next version takes a slightly different approach with behaviours being:

- Continued;
- Increased; or
- Decreased.

Known as CID objectives, these are less commonly used.

The terms 'target' and 'objective' are often used interchangeably. However, we usually regard a target as being measurable, often using calculations and numbers, whereas an objective may be recorded using language, being observed and assessed rather than measured. Some targets lend themselves to measurement, whilst professional development objectives do not. The latter lend themselves more readily to the observation and assessment of changes in behaviour.

Targets can often fail if:

- the targets are too focused on process – it is easier if they are focused on outcomes;
- outcome targets are not linked to other planning;
- team leaders set too many targets, as this causes overload;
- targets are to comfortable, historic or unlikely to be attainable;
- they are linked to the wrong or poor strategy;
- the psychology of target setting is wrong; or
- targets are not followed through.

Other blockages to target achievement may relate to fear of failure, others' reactions, fear of risk, or lack of visualisation. The reasons for not achieving targets are many and varied; a process of review and improvement will enable target setting to become more effective year on year. It does not matter what you call targets/objectives, how you agree them, record them, monitor them or observe, assess or measure them, so long as the process works for the staff and clients. I find targets or objectives need to relate to the role and team member in general, the whole job and the competence profile. If targets or objectives are linked only to hard, client- or profit-based outcomes, motivation is reduced.

Impact on your team?

If you use the performance-coaching process with professionalism, skill, insight and genuine intent it could prove to be a key tool in moving your team and organisation from being a series of processes, structures and separate groups of individuals to being an effective, flexible and focused team/learning organisation. In the hands of leaders with vision, performance coaching can help create learning organisations that transform the attitudes, knowledge and skills of staff and clients. If you see the value of performance coaching, you can see it not as separate or in addition to the core function of the organisation, teams or individuals or an isolated function, but as a flexible, yet systematic, professional process that enables and support continuous improvement through professional development. The organisational learning that takes place as a result of performance coaching helps align and enhance the capacity of individuals and teams in order to meet the agreed aims, objectives and vision of the organisation. Where the performance-coaching process is working well there is a direct linkage between progress targets, professional development targets, action plans and the development plan; one informs the other in a cycle of growth and development.

Impact on you?

Have a second go at the self-review and see if any learning has taken place.

Performance coaching should be:	Yes/Partly/No
Integrated and inform staff development, target setting and development/improvement/business planning.	
A structured professional dialogue based on objective data, information, work observations and appraisee self-review.	
Seen as being a key tool in helping your team focus on their core professional or business tasks.	
Transparent, rational, sustainable, low in bureaucracy and allows for unforeseen issues and problems that arise mid-year.	
Reviewed regularly by the users of the process with suggestions for improvement being accepted by senior staff, if feasible.	
Score: Yes = 2, Partly = 1, No = 0. **The fewer points scored out of 10, the more you need to update your knowledge of effective performance management.**	

How did you rate yourself second time round? This all takes a good deal of thinking about so, if you cannot see how this might work in your organisation, give yourself some time to reflect and start slowly and modestly. Remember that a journey of a thousand miles begins with the first step; have faith!

Further reading

Byham, C. and Cox, J, (1998) *Zapp: The Lightning of Empowerment.* London: Century Business.

Carnell, E. (2006) 'Mentoring, coaching and learning: examining the connections', *Professional Development Today*, spring: 10–16.

Catholic Education Service (2000) *Performance Management in Catholic Schools.* Nottingham: Midland Regional Printers.

Cordingley, P. (2006) 'Coaching and mentoring: a national framework?' *Professional Development Today*, spring: 7–9.

Creasy, J. and Paterson, F. (2005) *Leading Coaching in Schools.* Nottingham: National College for School Leadership.

Department for Education and Employment (DfEE) (2000a) *Performance Management in Schools: Model Performance Management Policy.* London: The Stationery Office.

Department for Education and Employment (DfEE) (2000b) *Performance Management in Schools: Performance Management Framework.* DfEE 0051/2000. London: The Stationery Office.

Drucker, P. (1986) *The Frontiers of Management.* London: Heinemann.

Handy, C. (1989) *The Age of Unreason.* London: Arrow Business Books.

Johnson, J. (1998) *Who Moved My Cheese?* New York: G. P. Putnam's Sons.

Jones, J. (2006) 'Coaching for better staff performance', *Professional Development Today*, spring: 17–23.

Joy, B. (2006) 'Trained mentor-coaches – making a difference', *Professional Development Today*, spring: 38–45.

Lawson, I. (1999) *Leaders for Tomorrow's Society.* London: The Industrial Society.

McGrane, J. (2006) 'Does coaching make a difference?', *Professional Development Today*, spring: 124–8.

Miliband, D. (2003) 'School improvement and performance management', speech to the Performance Management Conference, Bournemouth. Available from info@dfes.gsi.gov.uk.

Mintzberg, H. (1973) *The Nature of Managerial Work.* New York: HarperCollins.

Pedler, M, Burgoyne, J, and Boydell, T. (1991) *The Learning Company; A Strategy for Sustainable Development.* Maidenhead: McGraw-Hill.

Peters, T. and Waterman, R. (1982) *In Search of Excellence.* New York and London: Harper and Row.

Senge, P.M. (1990) *The Fifth Discipline: The Age and Practice of the Learning Organization.* London: Century Press.

Wellins, R. Byham, W. and Wilson, J. (1991) *Empowered Teams.* San Francisco, CA: Jossey-Bass.

Motivating your team

This chapter is about:

What it takes to be a team leader in a variety of settings in different organisations. I offer an overview of what it takes to be a team leader in any context. I look at theory and practice and illustrate the learning points with scenarios. You also get an opportunity to undertake a self-review at the beginning and end of the chapter, to assess its impact on your mindset, skills and knowledge.

Why is this important?

An ancient Chinese proverb tells us, 'a journey of a thousand miles begins with a single step'. The journey of organisational, team and personal improvement begins with a single step also; the trick is to ensure that first step is taken in the right direction! As an effective team leader you can play a key role in helping to align and attune the potential, aspirations and talents of your staff as individuals, and as a team, with vision and direction of your organisation. If you get the role of team leader right you can help your team develop a sense of purpose and direction in their roles, allowing them to realise their own dreams whilst functioning effectively within the constraints around them. Your well-chosen efforts as team leader can be transformational for your organisation, your team and the individuals in it.

Self-review

Before you go any further why not undertake this brief self-review to help you assess your level of awareness in relation to the role of team leader. Answer each question in turn with a Yes or Partly or No response. When you have read this chapter, repeat the self-review again and note any progress or further development needs.

A team leader should:	Yes/Partly/No
Have a tight control of the team at all times, knowing in detail what is going on.	
Leave the team to organise itself and just expect the team members to get on with the job.	
Focus on the output and targets of the team and not concern him or herself with any personal issues or concerns.	
Treat all members of the team the same way in order to ensure fairness and equal opportunities.	
Ignore office, department and staffroom politics.	

Score: Yes = 2, Partly = 1, No = 0.
The fewer points scored out of 10 the better. The more points scored, the more you need to update your knowledge of leading teams effectively.

Good practice

As an effective team leader you can help your team know what the issues are, what people think, how effective they are, where they want to get to, how to get there and how they fit into the big picture of organisational needs. This is the essence of effective team leadership, motivation and performance coaching.

Case study

When Liz arrived at her new workplace she expected to work as the secretary, she had no idea that eventually she would end up on the leadership team as Business/Practice Manager leading her own team. Now Liz is fully involved in the development-planning and performance-coaching process and is the first member of the support staff to serve as a senior leader.

(Continued)

How did Liz get to become a member of the leadership team and leader of her own team?

After several years of performance review with her team leader, it became clear that Liz was a very able secretary, fast at typing, used shorthand, was organised and had ideas of her own, and she was content in her role. After some time Liz was encouraged to take on more responsibility and support the professional staff in as many ways as possible, in terms of administrative, facilities, resource and financial support. As a result of her expanded role, Liz undertook a job re-evaluation and was then promoted from Secretary to Administrative Officer, but she never was an administrator by nature. Liz had ideas about how to improve the office, facilities, resource and finance management. She had no problem in letting other staff know of her ideas and views. After some encouragement from her boss and chair of the board, Liz decided to undertake a business management course. Upon completion of the course, Liz had a nationally recognised certificate delivered by Manchester Metropolitan University. Liz was asked to expand her role even further and she was again encouraged to redesign and re-evaluate her workload and that of Sally, the part-time secretary. Liz now serves on the Senior Leadership Team (SLT) as Business Manager and leads her own team: the resource and finance team. Sally is now the Administrator. Liz manages and appraises most of the support staff.

Liz knows the needs of the organisation in terms of its core processes and she is able to align the talents and work of her team and organisational resources to help meet those needs. The role Liz now has is key in the effectiveness of the organisation; her efforts support the professional staff in their efforts to support the clients. The role Liz now plays, as Business Manager, motivates her as she is leading processes she understands. This change also motivates the senior professional staff as they are now able to focus on their preferred tasks of dealing with staff and clients; a win-win scenario.

Now Liz meets annually with Sally, Tony (site manager) and the support staff, to review their work, their targets and their professional development needs. She attempts to align the work of her team with that of the rest of the organisation. She meets with her team mid-year to review progress and hear about any issues they have. Now she is growing into the role of coach for her team, this does not come easily to Liz as she has been very hands on and personally efficient for many years. As Business Manager, she now has so many tasks to manage she can no longer do them all in person, so she is quickly developing the process of delegation

(Continued)

(Continued)

and coaching. This is not an easy process for somebody who is relatively new to the coaching aspect of performance management and team leadership, but she is finding it rewarding and effective.

With the aid of an effective team leader, who spotted her potential and talent, Liz is now a senior member of staff in the organisation, an organisation that is good at 'growing', motivating and coaching other leaders in-house. Liz has grown as a professional and as an individual. This was a transformational change and very motivating for her, all as a result of performance coaching linked to effective training and development.

Ask yourself if your role as team leader is regarded as a key role in your organisation? Is there a clear linkage between development planning, the appraisal meeting, target setting, data analysis, work observation and professional development? If there is not, should there be if your people are the most expensive and vital resource you have? As team leader your role is vital, whether you are a senior manager, middle manager, office manager or business manager. You need to have an overview of the processes in place, an appropriate attitude and suitable skills and knowledge.

Getting started

Before getting to grips with the detail of the role of team leader, I provide an overview of the philosophy and attitudes that need to be in place for performance coaching to be really effective.

To be an effective performance coach you will need to consider the following eight steps:

1   Learn to single-task.
2   Develop a cool head and warm heart.
3   Create a positive culture and climate.
4   Coach your team.
5   Have a well-managed performance process.
6   Realise that rational use of data and management information motivates.
7   Align and attune professional development and training.
8   Keep it effective by continuous improvement.

Let me explain these steps in a little more detail.

1   Learn to single-task

If you want to help change others first change yourself. If you are going to become an effective and credible team leader you need the right mindset before you develop the right skill set. The first step that needs to be taken, in ensuring you are effective in your context, is to examine your own motives, intentions concerns, drives and leadership qualities. As a team leader you will almost certainly become involved in the organisation's performance-coaching process, the key process in motivating and harnessing the effectiveness of colleagues and co-workers. The performance-coaching process I illustrate in this book will use detailed observation and performance data relating to the individuals in your team. *These are sharp instruments!* Sharp instruments of any kind should be used professionally, wisely, carefully and with compassion. Sharp instruments can be used to heal or damage. The instrument itself is neutral; it is the attitude and intention of the user that is key. When dealing with a team member in a one-to-one coaching situation become an expert serial single-tasker. Stop multi-tasking when dealing with fellow human beings on a one-to-one basis. Give your team member your full attention!

2   Develop a cool head and warm heart

In a practical sense, how do you, as a leader gain enough respect from your people for your role as team leader in an effective performance-coaching process to be of benefit to the organisation and the individuals in your team? Clearly it helps if you are good at your job, if your skills and knowledge are sufficient and if you are experienced and professional. However, for your role as team leader to be really valued and transformational your deeper motives and competencies need to be evident to staff. If your staff are to talk to you about their weaknesses, their concerns, their aspirations and their vision then trust must be in place. Trust is the vital element in the relationship between team leader and those they aspire to lead. If your people do not trust you on several levels, they will not be inclined to follow you, and a leader without followers is a leader in name only. These deeper and more personal competencies and qualities are often referred to as 'emotional intelligence'. Without a sufficient degree of understanding of yourself and your team as people, no formal training in team leadership or performance coaching is going to make you effective. To be a trusted team leader you need to understand your team and yourself, and you need a 'warm heart' so your team recognise you value them as individuals. This level of communication is not easy to teach. You also need a cool head as you need to be clear about the process you are involved in, its benefits and limitations. If you are unclear as to why and how the process is to run, what chance is there of motivated but busy staff buying into it? If you see your team leader role as a bolt-on process, taking you away from your core tasks, then you are destined to fail. You need to be confident of the purposes you are using in your role as team leader and you need to be confident of your motives; seeking to align and develop the aspirations and talents of your people, not to monitor and control. It is not enough to 'care' you also need to be well organised and manage your team well if you are to motivate them fully. A well-organised performance process can become transformational for you, your team and the organisation; a process that literally enables people to examine the needs of the organisation and themselves. This can lead to change if handled well by a skilled team leader.

3   Create a positive culture and climate

You know from experience that it is not easy to get someone to change their behaviour or habits. This is human nature. If you accept the fact that, except in extreme circumstances, people change themselves, then you will have taken the first step in creating a culture and climate in which your team members can develop themselves. You will move away from needing to control, and realise it is not you making people change; instead you are creating the conditions for people to change themselves in a positive manner. If you want a plant to grow, you place it in fertile soil, feed and water it, protect it from the extremes of the elements and then it will grow on its own. This is a mindset that will help an effective culture and climate grow in your workplace. 'When an organisation [and team] has developed sufficiently well a less hands on style of leadership will need to be adopted, one which empowers and develops other leaders in the organisation. The process of letting go of the reins of control can be very painful for leaders who prefer the hands on approach' (Rowan and Taylor, 2002: 12). Once your team is starting to become effective you also need to allow them to lead. You may set limits and delegate carefully, but you cannot control a highly effective team. If you do they will only ever move at your pace and think with one perspective. This urge to control must be addressed and you will need to accept that you are no longer at the forefront of every development. In this your team will be able to develop a degree of flair and self-motivation. I touch on this aspect of team control in other chapters as this is vital to the motivation of good quality team members.

4   Coach your team

I have observed that the best leaders and managers go through phases or stages of leadership development. Managers and leaders who are less reflective may stay in one stage of leadership. Initially many leaders lead or manage everything because they find it hard to delegate; I call this the Hero phase. Eventually a leader may move into the Hub phase where he/she does not need to lead or manage all key tasks but will delegate, even if delegation is a little tight. The final phase a mature and confident leader or manager may enter is that of Heretic. In this phase, the coaching phase, the team is steered and coached by a series of questions rather than instructions. In an open and fast-changing learning culture the team leader is not only a manager or supervisor, but also a coach. If you lead a large department or office, you may have many people who report to you or your managers. If this is the case, you may need to develop other team leaders within your department, therefore, you may need to coach them.

Coaching is very demanding, so it may be wise to attempt to coach or appraise only a few colleagues at any one time, although there are no hard and fast rules in relation to the size of your team or the number of people you coach. Your organisation or profession may have regulations in relation to team size based on the particular context you work in, so you may need to be aware of these regulations. There is no single context that is common to all organisations, businesses or professions, so you will need to make arrangements that fit your particular context. It is for you, your leaders and your staff to design a process and structure that works in your context. The key is that you know your team member and their work. Another ancient Chinese proverb says, 'it doesn't matter what colour the cat is so long as it catches mice'. Design your system to match your context. I discuss the issue of 'team leader as coach' in other chapters.

The concepts outlined so far go beyond the notion of line management, the role and processes suggested being more of a coaching role, suitable for a professional context where staff are regarded as colleagues. In this professional context you are likely to have staff who want to engage. If you have staff who are causing problems or not competent, then the performance coaching process should be suspended and other procedures brought into place – disciplinary or competency procedures for example. With colleagues who are professional in their approach you will be able to act as a coach in the performance process. You will be able to work with your staff to help them develop their own strategies to move themselves and their work forward. In coaching mode you will not be at the centre of all developments and you will not be the source of all knowledge and power, as you will recognise that your key role is to empower and motivate your staff within the context of the needs of the organisation.

5 *Have a well-managed performance process*

As your motivation and performance processes become more effective, aligned and integrated, your organisation will hold the gathering and analysis of data and information as key. This data and information then informs the cycle of planning, monitoring and review which then informs the improvement/development plan. As your skills and capabilities in relation to performance coaching become more proficient, the process will move from being a once a year event to being the key process in understanding the organisation, and co-ordinating and maximising the talents and aspirations of staff. An effective performance-coaching process will impact powerfully on the organisation's climate, culture and results.

Unless your organisation or your professional regulations dictate the timing and the format of the appraisal/review meeting, it is best designed to suit your staff and the context of your organisation. Usually there is one appraisal meeting a year where performance to date is reviewed and recorded. This may involve the review of targets or objectives. Within the same meeting there will usually be discussion about the future work, aspirations and needs of the individual, again the key elements of this discussion being recorded during the meeting. The final phase of the meeting is addressing strategies to move the individual on, which may be recorded as targets or objectives. It is quite possible for the meeting to take no more than 60 to 75 minutes. This meeting is best held in quality time and in a quiet and comfortable room. It is common for the records of the appraisal to be completed and signed by both parties during the meeting. It is also useful if the appraisee can add a comment in relation to their agreement (or not) with the results of the meeting. Whilst the coaching method attempts to engage and motivate staff to take the lead role in their own appraisal, it needs to be recognised that there will be times when the appraiser and appraisee disagree. In such case you may have to stand your ground and, if necessary, refer the appraisee to the appeals procedure.

6   Realise that rational use of data and management information motivates

Experienced colleagues are unlikely to be motivated to change unless you move away from opinion, towards offering evidence that identifies behaviours and management information that is accepted by the appraisee. If 'a journey of a thousand miles begins with a single step', then it seems logical and professional to ensure that first we know where we are, than that the first step is taken in the right direction, we have an appropriate destination in mind, we know where we are when we arrive and we can offer evidence to prove it! For your performance-coaching and organisational-improvement processes to be effective you will need to hold the gathering and analysis of data, information and work/task observation as key. Reflection on such objective data forms the basis of good management information, which in turn forms the basis of knowledge relating to the organisation and the individuals within it. Quality data, information and knowledge underpin and inform the appraisal interview, which in turn informs professional development, coaching and support of individuals and teams. The cycle of planning, monitoring and review informs the development plan and various action plans. This is the basis of an integrated performance-coaching process.

To have an effective performance and improvement process you may also need to gather what some may refer to as softer data and information relating to the informal systems and relationships – what some refer to as the shadow side of the organisation. Quite simply the effective use of hard and soft, but valid, data motivates staff if used properly as part of a structured professional dialogue designed to help staff in their core tasks. The process needs to be professional, logical, intelligent and sustainable, not bureaucratic, and needs to be integrated with the other processes of the organisation.

7   Align and attune professional development and training

If you use the performance-coaching process to gather quality management information you will see the process is not separate or in addition to the core function of the organisation, teams and individuals, but is a flexible, yet systematic, professional process that enables and supports continuous improvement through professional development. The organisational learning that takes place as a result of performance coaching should be clear, with a direct linkage between appraisal/review, professional development, action plans and the development/improvement plan; one informs the other in a cycle of growth and development. In this process the professional development of staff is not a series of events taking place off site, but clearly identified strategies owned by the appraisee and linked to his/her needs and aspirations. Much of this development may take the form of in-house coaching and support which often proves to be very cost-effective if done well. If undertaken well, as a result of review and reflection, this integrated approach to coaching and training, tailored to the needs of the organisation, teams and individuals, can lead to profound and systemic change that goes well beyond the quick fix of some off-site courses. Professional development becomes very focused and specific to the needs of individuals and teams so they can function effectively, with motivation, in order to help the organisation serve its clients.

8   Keep it effective by continuous improvement

It is vital to review and improve all systems and processes, because they soon become demotivators if they are no longer effective or sustainable. A process of continuous improvement by small steps should be developed by the users of the process; referred to as 'kaizen' by Japanese quality managers. This kaizen process can offer evolution not revolution and can help turn a slow-moving school or company into a 'learning organisation'. To keep the performance and motivation processes effective, at least annually ask your team what they think of the process. You may ask, 'What went well?' (WWW). Let staff comment that it could be 'even better if' (EBI) we did this or that as an improvement. This need not be a complex task; it may not even involve staff meeting formally to review the process. In a mature organisation you could put a flip chart in a prominent place in the office and divide the chart into two vertical columns, one headed WWW and the other EBI. Once your staff get used to this kaizen process it can be used by you to review all sorts of processes. In this way your performance management process will continue to be linked to school/organisation improvement and continue to be valued as practical, sustainable and relevant by those involved.

Impact on your team?

There are many academic and business theories of motivation, too many for me to go into here. Clearly if your team is physically, psychologically or emotionally unsafe as a result of poor management or leadership, it is unlikely to be motivated by performance-coaching processes no matter how useful you make them. These basic human needs must to be in place if your team is to perform well and be motivated by your team leadership skills.

As suggested earlier it is motivating for team members, team leaders and senior staff to see and assess the impact of processes used. Your context will be different to those found in other organisations but the notion of evidencing motivation and performance applies no matter what business or profession you are in.

Impact on you?

What do you think you have gained from reading this chapter? Something of real use? Why not return to the self-evaluation exercise you did at the beginning of the chapter and see if your thoughts, knowledge or attitudes have changed.

Answer each question in turn with a Yes or Partly or No.

A team leader should:	Yes/Partly/No
Have a tight control of the team at all times, knowing in detail what is going on.	
Leave the team to organise itself and just expect the team members to get on with the job.	
Focus on the output and targets of the teams and not concern him or herself with any personal issues or concerns.	

(Continued) Treat all members of the team the same way in order to ensure fairness and equal opportunities.	
Ignore office, department and staffroom politics.	
Score: Yes = 2, Partly = 1, No = 0. The fewer points scored out of 10 the better. The more points scored, the more you need to update your knowledge of leading teams effectively.	

Reflect on what I have said and then apply the concepts you value in your business or profession, see if the change has any impact. I think you will find the changes you make of benefit, I certainly did when I applied them in my organisation, a school, which is full of people of varying skills, experience, qualifications and motivation – no easy place to lead.

Further reading

Adair, J. (2006) *Headship and Motivation*. London: Kogan Page.

Argyris, C. (1978) 'A leadership dilemma: skilled incompetence'; in co Argyris and D. Schon, *Organisational Learning: A Theory of Action Perspective*. London: Addison-Wesley.

Argyris, C. and Schon, D. (1974) *Theory in Practice: Increasing Professional Effectiveness*. San Francisco, CA: Jossey-Bass.

Boyatzis, R. (1999) 'Self-directed change and learning as a necessary meta-competency for success and effectiveness in the twenty-first century', in R. Sims and J. Veres (eds), *Keys to Employee Success in Coming Decades*. westport, CT: Quorum Books.

Caldwell, B. and Spinks, J. (1992) *Leading the Self Managing School*. London: Falmer Press.

Cockman, P., Evans, B. and Reynolds, P. (1999) *Consulting for Real People*. Maidenhead: McGraw-Hill.

Covey, S. (1989) *The Seven Habits of Highly Effective People*. New York: Simon and Schuster.

Egan, G. (1993) *Adding Value: A Systematic Guide to Business Driven Management and Leadership*. San Francisco, CA: Jossey-Bass.

Evans, R. (1998) *The Human Side of School Change*. San Francisco, CA: Jossey-Bass.

Garret, B. (1990) *Creating a Learning Organisation*. Hemel Hempstead: Director Books, Fitzwilliam.

Gold, A., Evans, J., Early, P., Halpin, D. and Collarbone, P. (2003) 'Principled principals?', *Educational Management and Administration*, 31(2): 127–38.

Goleman, D. (1998) *Working with Emotional Intelligence*. London: Bloomsbury.

Goleman, D. (2003) *Destructive Emotions and How We Can Overcome Them*. London: Bloomsbury.

Hammer, M. and Champy, J. (1994) *Reengineering the Corporation. London:* Nicholas Brealey.

Nonaka, I. and Takeuchi, H. (1995) *The Knowledge Creating Company*: *How Japanese Companies Create the Dynamic of Innovation.* New York: Oxford University Press.

Osterman, K. and Kottkamp, R. (1994) 'Rethinking professional development,' in N. Bennett, R. Glatter and R. Levacic (eds), *Improving Educational Management.* London: Paul Chapman Publishing.

Parkin, M. (2001) *Coaching and Storytelling.* London: Kogan Page.

Reading, M. (2003) 'Still on the cycle', *Management in Education*, 16(5): 17–23.

Schein, E. (1984) 'Coming to a new awareness of organizational culture'. *Sloan Management Review*, 25(2): 3–16.

Senge, P. (1990) *The Fifth Discipline.* London: Nicholas Brealey.

Senge, P., Lucas, T. and Dutton, J. (2000) *Schools that Learn.* London: Nicholas Brealey.

Wellins, R., Byham, W. and Wilson, J. (1991) *Empowered Teams.* San Francisco, CA: Jossey-Bass.

Motivation and continuous improvement

This chapter is about:

Continuous improvement and how it can be used to remove blockages to performance coaching, the 'demotivators', and replace them with processes and procedure that foster and promote motivation and effective performance coaching.

Why is it important?

If you want your team to be effective, perform well and be motivated without it damaging those involved, you need to know about sustainable continuous improvement processes and techniques. If you want to avoid the sort of revolutionary change that crashes into your organisation and your team, you need to read on. If you value evolution rather than revolution then this is the chapter for you. If you like chaos and thrive on the adrenaline of shock treatment then you will not like what is on offer in this chapter but I would suggest you need to learn from this chapter more than any other.

Self-review

Now you want to read about motivation and continuous improvement. Well, before you do read on I think you need to check the climate of your organisation. With a poor climate very little motivation and continuous improvement will take place. Reading this book to this point should have had a positive impact on your knowledge in relation to what constitutes a positive learning climate designed to promote motivation and effective performance in your organisation. Complete this self-evaluation now, and at the end of the chapter complete it again to help you assess the impact of the content of this chapter on your learning.

Measuring the learning climate in your organisation		
There is little encouragement to learn new skills and abilities.	1 2 3 4 5	People are encouraged to extend themselves and their knowledge.
People are secretive; information is hoarded.	1 2 3 4 5	People share their views and information.
People are ignored and then blamed when things go wrong.	1 2 3 4 5	People are recognised for good work and rewarded for learning.
People are not paid to think; their ideas are not valued.	1 2 3 4 5	Efforts are made to get people to share their ideas.
People do not help each other or share resources.	1 2 3 4 5	People are helpful; pleasure is taken in the success of others.
How well did you score? The higher you score the more your organisation is likely to be a learning organisation with a positive climate for growth, improvement and motivation.		

Good practice

Scenario

Peter was preparing himself for a meeting with his team. He thought he was well prepared and so far this had been a pretty ordinary day. As he arrived in the meeting his team were in good spirits and so was Peter. This was a good team and Peter rated them highly. Generally they were hard-working, creative and usually quite outspoken. The organisation had a positive policy of protecting its people from unnecessary work overload and they were all aware of work–life balance. This team had also fully internalised the notion of what they called kaizen, which was their shorthand for 'continuous improvement by small steps brought about by the user of the process or procedure'. Clearly kaizen is easier than that mouthful! Peter was an advocate of kaizen and had built this approach into all

(Continued)

that went on in the organisation; even social events are reviewed! Bearing in mind this approach and that this organisation had won many awards and was generally regarded as 'outstanding' in term of improvement and performance, what could possible come up at the meeting that would surprise Peter and his colleagues?

As usual Peter and his team were analysing and exploring a particular issue and, again as usual, his team had plenty of views in relation to the matter in hand. This team had an unrelenting focus on performance of all kinds, but improvement and output performance in relation to their clients' well-being was their main focus in this debate. When Peter asked what it was that was hindering quick and effective improvement of their processes, one of the team members suggested unnecessary paperwork was part of the problem. At this point Peter did not really understand the response as he hates unnecessary paperwork and is well known for it. Peter did a little more digging and tried to understand more precisely what the problem was. Then came the surprise, not enough to be called a shock but certainly a learning point had emerged for Peter. His team went to explain what it was they regarded as the unhelpful and unnecessary paperwork they had to complete. Peter could not believe his ears, he had never seen or heard of this paperwork yet most of his team dutifully filled it in on a regular basis! Being a hard-working and loyal bunch, the team had completed these forms for years and never really seen the use of them. The team had not complained or refused to fill the forms in, but had just done the task and moved on to more important things, like making sure their clients were well looked after. In other words they had focused on their key task despite the paperwork that seemed purposefully designed to stop them being effective.

Peter asked his team to explain the mystery paperwork to him, its purpose and its origin, as clearly Peter had not been party to its design – yet he had been the leader of the organisation for quite a few years. The staff took time to explain the paperwork to Peter but when he asked what its purpose and effectiveness was they had no reply. Peter asked who had designed and implemented the paperwork, again no reply. Next Peter and his team discussed the possibility that the paperwork may be the type of unhelpful paperwork organisations have to complete for local or central government but again no reply. Peter asked his team why they completed the paperwork, and every single member of the team, including other members of the leadership team replied, 'Because we thought you found it useful boss!' At that point the team took the joint decision to research the paperwork issue further to ensure it was needed for some obscure reason. After some reflection the team decided to not complete the paperwork for a trial period and low and behold the removal of the paperwork task only had a positive and motivational impact on the team.

So what was the learning from all this for Peter and the team? It may seem obvious, but the team needed to learn to question everything at regular intervals and then speak up if a process was unhelpful or unneeded. The team has found that if they question as a team they can constantly review and improve processes and procedures at work. This does not give freedom for individuals to take unilateral action and simply stop using a process or procedure. Decisions need to be discussed, reflected upon and tested, but this need not be a long process. In this way Peter's team stay motivated, focused on their key roles and tasks, and manage to maintain a reasonable work–life balance as they are not being asked by an unthinking leadership team to complete tasks that are unnecessary and unhelpful.

Getting started

The process of regular review of policies, procedure and performance, or continuous improvement, started modestly in Peter's organisation. Slowly, by a process of regular review and improvement, 'kaizen,' the organisation moved from revolutionary change to a process of evolutionary change. This may be open to academic or theological debate but it seems to me evolution has a habit of making organisations (and organisms) better adapted to their surroundings in an almost imperceptible way. It seems to me that evolutions also have mostly beneficial changes in the short and long term. Revolutions usually have passionate and charismatic people at their outset and injured or damaged people at their conclusion. If the process of change in organisations can be evolutionary, I have found, there is less resistance and more team members openly add their ideas, dreams and talents, thereby creating a change that is owned by the team with minimal damage to the organisation and the people linked to it. At times we all get caught up in the 'winds of change', and we may even get caught up in a revolution caused by others, but I have found it best to keep internal revolution to a minimum and expend your energies on meeting the needs of the client and your team members.

I will offer one further scenario before I move on, as I think this also illustrates the need constantly to be vigilant about unnecessary rule-creeping in even the best organisations.

Scenario

Peter was yet again surprised by the creeping burden of unnecessary and unhelpful processes and procedures. This time Peter is working with a group of clients in a quality circle. These quality circles are held three times

(Continued)

a year and are the times when a group of representative clients come together with Peter and the organisation's business manager to discuss the effectiveness of the organisation from the point of view of the client. The clients were offering their opinions in relation to the issues under review when one of them asked a question about one of the regulations followed in the catering area. The clients explained the regulation and the two leaders (Peter and Liz) listened. The clients are used to offering solutions to their own problems at these meetings, so Peter and Liz listened on. This time Peter was ready as he had dealt with a case of creeping and unnecessary regulations a few years earlier (the paperwork scenario). This time he was not quite so surprised when the clients outlined a whole series of rules and regulation linked to eating in the canteen. It came as no shock to hear that, as if by some mystical process that has a life of its own, a series of small but irritating rules had evolved.

Peter went into kaizen mode and the meeting reviewed the rule in relation to the canteen and then identified the rules that were clearly useful for effectiveness or safety reasons. They also identified several rules that seemed to have no real logic or need. These rules were noted in the minutes and a period of investigation arranged. Key staff were interviewed – other school leaders, team members, catering staff, cooks and so on – but nobody seemed to know where the unhelpful rules came from or when they were introduced. Yet again Peter was told that staff thought the rules were his!

The organisation ran for a while without the bogus rules and yet again the result was motivating for all involved. The catering is more relaxed and less congested, and the clients are happier with the provision.

The learning for Peter and the team is not only to encourage staff to question unhelpful procedures and processes, but actually encourage your clients to do the same. I have nearly always found it useful to ask staff and clients what the blockages are in the organisation. If I ask staff and clients to offer solutions to the blockages they have identified, they nearly always come up with great suggestions. We now listen and reflect on the suggestions made, we assess risk or liability and then 'pilot' the new process or procedure. After a very brief review we adopt the new process or procedure and add it to our record of collective wisdom, our procedure manual.

The kaizen review

Perhaps by now you are asking how we manage to review so many things so often without this being negative, time-consuming and demotivating? The

What went well	Even better if

Figure 4.1 *Flip chart review sheet template*

answer is that for virtually all reviews we do not organise a meeting or hold any formal or structured discussion. Formal review and discussion is only timetabled for a quality circle meeting if our usual and informal process does not work for some reason or if it throws up issues that are worthy/complex enough to merit discussion. Quite simply, what we do after most events, or the use of a process such as the performance coaching and review meetings, is put a flip chart on the wall in the staff rest area and ask for comments relating to 'What went well?' and 'even better if'. The flip chart is set out as in Figure 4.1.

I have included (in Figure 4.2) a review sheet completed by staff, in passing, when this flip chart was left on the wall of their rest area soon after a school social/fund-raising event. I use this type of event to show that we do not only

Fund-raising/social event	
What went well	**Better next time**
• Well led, 'quiet' but effective from Chair and committee • Activities fine • Tidy up in record time (the few helpers were very helpful) • Good atmosphere – very cheerful • Hamper event very popular • Organisers very organised in week before the event	• Staff to ensure all children have an adult with them – no children allowed to attend unless with adult (18+) (unless helping a member of staff who will take care of this child) • Doors need to be more secure to stop lone children entering (change code) • Close staff car park gate to stop casual parking (and blocking it) to allow staff access and emergency service access • Guests coming in pre-6 p.m. opening time • Free refreshments (drink etc.) for volunteers • Treasurer's to be in a more secure part of the building

Figure 4.2 *Completed flip chart review sheet*

review 'professional' processes but all significant or complex processes including social and fund-raising events involving clients and staff.

This document would be passed to key members of the event committee and key staff in the organisation. The point would be actioned and then used to improve the event or reduce the demotivating factors that are linked to it. You can see some of the points raised are quite detailed and low key, but we find the low-key issues irritate over the period of several events if they are not rectified. This process and thinking applies equally well to the review of the performance processes in the organisation.

Next I offer an old version of the review sheet (Figure 4.3). This version we used for many years. You will notice there are three boxes in this review flip chart. There is still a 'What went well?' but the other two boxes are 'Not so well' and 'Better next time'. We found three questions worked well but the current chart only has two and works even better. One reason for this improvement, a kaizen of our kaizen process you might say, is that busy staff tended to offer a 'moan' in the 'Not so well' box and then not offer a suggestion directly linked to it in the 'Better next time' box.

The process we use now, the two-box process, makes staff offer a suggestion linked to their concern and it puts it in the positive form of 'it would be "even better if" we improved the process by … '. Some of the points contained in

Fund-raising and social event	
Went well	**Not so well**
• Good number of activities • Very well organised by the committee • Good fun – easy	• Audience for the race event has dwindled • Short on volunteer helpers • Busy time of year • Kitchen floor sticky and trays that had been borrowed were not wiped clean
Better next time	
• Have race event before the main event opens; spectators would not dwindle and may get more offers of help from volunteers • Fun races before sprint • Medals at finish of the race event • Move this social event to a better time of year • Ensure all areas and items used are cleaned • More volunteer helpers asked in advance of the event	

Figure 4.3 *Previous version of flip chart review sheet*

the review seem quite basic but I have often found good quality staff are demotivated by silly, seemingly insignificant, frustrations; for example being blocked in the car park at the end of a long day when they have volunteered to help and now they have to rush off to pick up their child from a carer!

Removing blockages

There exists a lot of theory relating to motivation, much of it very useful and practical, so I do not intend to run through the theory as you probably know of most of it, or at least you know where the book is on your shelf. I intend to be practical and helpful in relation to the removal of blockages and offer some comment linked to what I find in my own role and in my own life.

Basically if you undertake this process of review with your team, your clients and some of your key stakeholders, you will hear their concerns and, if you manage it properly, their solutions. You are not bound by what you hear, so why not ask and listen? In terms of your team, why do you go through the complex, time-consuming and expensive process of recruiting new team members who are well qualified and/or experienced, then refuse to listen to them? Many team members seem to be content if you, as team leader, at least listen to them! If you actually understand their concerns and act on them you will be motivating them even further; this is not rocket science. When you do free up your processes and you do start to listen to their comment and solutions you will have 'ignited the blue touch paper on a firework'. You may have to stand back and watch it go off at times for your own safety. When you become more experienced at leading by igniting talent rather than dampening it, you will start to learn the colours and burntime of your 'fireworks' and will orchestrate a superb show. This takes bravery and skill, but you would not put on much of a display if you were the only firecracker in the box!

When you and your team get used to this process of review, discussion and change action, you may well be surprised by what it is that motivates and demotivates your people. I was. It may be that you think wages or hours worked are the big issues for them. To some degree these will be issues or blockages to motivation if the wages are so low that their standard of living is adversely affected. Long hours will also be a problem if the hours are unreasonable, damaging for health or managed in a way that means your team members too often have to let down family members and friends. I find my staff will put up with difficulties at work if they recognise it to be unavoidable. In fact I find, if the culture and climate of your organisation is generally positive, virtually all staff will put up with most difficulties. If the culture or climate is negative then even the smallest of difficulties causes problems. As team leader you are responsible for the attitude of your team and you have to find ways of motivating your team.

The blockages I have noticed when working as a team leader, a leader, a director and a consultant are often relatively minor in nature but major in impact. When people give their time and effort freely they expect a 'thank you'. This might sound silly but basic good manners and some sensitivity go a long way. One of the biggest blockages to goodwill and motivation could be you and the way you lead your team. You and the leadership styles you adopt have a huge impact on the goodwill of your team. If you learn to make sure nothing you do unconsciously blocks motivation, you will be at least halfway to being a good team leader.

Levers to motivation

Once you have removed as many blockages to motivation and performance as you can you might like to think about what it is that motivates your team and the individuals within it. I have found money is not the main motivator for most staff; some like responsibility, some freedom to operate, some the personal touch, others attaining goals and many a little recognition and praise for the work they have done. Some of these tools and techniques you can use are often referred to as 'levers'. Like a well-used lever in life, a well-used psychological lever can lift members of your team when they need to be lifted. You may think you do not have many levers to use with your staff, but reflect on this and then be creative. You will probably find you have more levers than you ever imagined. If you are successful, senior staff and your own team will almost certainly offer you more levers without you asking.

Scenario

Brenda was in need of a really good temporary member of staff to cover for a member of her team who had been promoted. The promotion was well deserved and to some degree expected but Brenda could not find another permanent, full-time member of staff in such a short time and it was vital to ensure the role was covered. Brenda asked one of the part-time team members (Joanne) if she would be able to step up to a full-time role for a while to help cover the vacant position. Joanne asked for time to discuss this with her partner, as there would be childcare implications. Brenda agreed to give Joanne time to discuss the offer with her family. Joanne was a very well respected and experienced member of the team and Brenda did not like to press Joanne too hard and risk damaging the goodwill Joanne showed on a regular basis.

Joanne returned the next day and told Brenda she could help but childcare was a problem. Brenda reminded Joanne that their organisation had childcare facilities for staff and Joanne could use them free of charge.

(Continued)

49

(Continued)

This seemed to put Joanne's mind at rest to some degree. Joanne then reminded Brenda that the she and her family had the holiday of a lifetime booked in the USA and working full time would cut into the holiday. Brenda had to think about this for a while, then she informed Joanne that there would be a way to work round that issue. If Joanne helped out for a few months Brenda would find a way to make sure Joanne and her family did not have to change holiday plans or even be rushed prior to the holiday. At that moment Brenda had no idea if the offers she had made would be easy to implement but it was clear Joanne was now ready to help out.

Joanne, with all her experience, training, knowledge and positive attitude, covered the post for twice as long as planned and did a superb job that was commented on by all staff, board members and clients. At the end of the cover period Joanne was offered flowers and public thanks at a well-attended event. She valued the childcare offered by Brenda; even more she enjoyed her family holiday and she very much appreciated the public thank you and flowers offered in recognition of her efforts.

Joanne is now back working part time and Brenda has managed to replace the original member of her team who was promoted. Joanne has helped with the induction of the new team member and provision for the clients has not been negatively impacted upon.

The trick is that Brenda was able to remove the blockages by using small and low-cost levers. Those levers were not listed in a manual; she just used her own initiative to solve the problem for the organisation, and it worked. Next Brenda was able to motivate Joanne with simple recognition, a genuine thank you and a bunch of flowers. Clearly, Brenda knew Joanne well and they trusted each other. This approach would need to be different for other staff who have different needs and motives. What the scenario illustrates is that Brenda knew which levers to use to motivate this particular team member, she did not allow details to stand in her way and she invented a lever or two to get the job done. Brenda works in public service so she is careful to work within guidelines and be informed by ethics but, in the end, being unimaginative, timid and rule-bound does not serve any client or team member well.

Review of impact and cost-effectiveness

Finally, I offer a few suggestions as to how you might review processes in a way that is a little more hard-nosed. I suggest the effectivenss of all training and development is reviewed. In-house training sessions are planned and reviewed upon completion. Courses, conferences or speakers are selected as appropriate. Review of external courses will also take place, with further training

Cost effective		Not cost effective	
Training, ½ day for 10 staff		Training course for 1 member of staff	
Staff satisfaction rating	90%	Individual satisfaction rating	45%
Travel time	0 hrs	Travel time	2 hrs
Trainer fee	£200 (½ day)	Course fee	£90 (½ day)
Staff travel	£00 (in house)	Staff travel	£16
Food	£50 (sandwiches)	Food	£0
Cover	£1200	Cover	£120
Total	£1450	Total	£226
Cost per person	£145	Cost per person	£226
Cosy-effectiveness rating		Cosy-effectiveness rating	
£145/90% = £1.61/percentage point		£226/45% = £5.22/percentage point	

Figure 4.4 *Example of a cost-effectiveness assessment of training*

planned if necessary. Individual training may be provided in-house or externally. Course application forms, and a pre-brief section of the in-house development review sheets, are completed prior to application for a course; these are submitted to the personnel team leader for approval. Upon completion of a course or development process, the review section of the development review sheet is completed and discussed with the personnel team leader, the debrief section is completed and signed by the team leader. The course advertisement and form are added to the individual's training and development file. The file is reviewed during performance coaching to ensure targets are being met and results forthcoming.

The cost-effectiveness of any training or development is broadly assessed by dividing the effectiveness rating with the cost, to give a cost per percentage point. The effectiveness of a programme is not only assessed at the end of a programme but after its impact has been assessed by performance coaching. In my organisation this process has thrown up some interesting data, with the cheaper, more local training events appearing inexpensive, but when staff cover costs, food, travel and so on are added they often produce low cost-effectiveness ratings. The apparently more expensive consultant or specific trainer, who is asked to come to an organisation to satisfy a specific need, often proves more cost-effective per person, per percentage point. An example of this is shown in Figure 4.4.

At first glance it would seem much cheaper to buy a course for £90 than pay a trainer costing more than twice as much to visit the organisation. Clearly there are economies of scale, and when you factor in satisfaction ratings the more expensive option seems even more effective. Even if the cost per person was identical, when you factor in the satisfaction rating this shows up the real cost/benefit of the training. This form of review is easy and paints an interesting picture when training provision is reviewed.

I find my staff rarely give courses a satisfaction rating that is as high as in-house training. Unless the courses are recognised as being very effective, they may well not deliver in the way promised. Often travel, parking and general wasting of time finding the venue reduces the rating as all of these factors are demotivators. In-house sessions usually deliver what the staff need/want and staff have less trouble with travel, parking, and so on.

This focus on what is cost-effective takes a little getting used to in an organisation that is used to ad hoc training with no follow-up, but the school has found this focus on what works has helped save time, goodwill and finances that can then be better spent on staff and pupils. Staff are motivated by being allowed to get on with their jobs and not having their time and goodwill wasted by attending meetings and training sessions that do not meet their individual needs or those of their team. To be effective and efficient takes thought, effort and procedures but in the end it pays off. Not only do staff get 'quality' time from the savings made but they usually get effective coaching and support, which enables them to be more effective in their roles. Finally on this point, it cannot be good to be careful professionals in relation to your craft/work but then be careless amateurs when it comes to the management of performance and professional development. In an organisation that believes in total quality, all products, recourses and services to staff, clients and board members should be as good as we could make them. I find really effective organisations do not settle for second best.

Impact on your team?

To start with it will take your team some time to get into the habit of continuous review and improvement. When they see the benefits of their reflections and suggestions, they will become motivated to take part. Eventually they will become good enough to review without the guidance of a team leader, as they will see the benefits for themselves as well as for the organisation. The organisation will evolve, keeping pace with change, in time moving ahead of change and into the area of innovation, and all based on the suggestions of your own team.

Impact on you?

So do you think the content of this chapter has had a positive impact on your knowledge in relation to what constitutes a positive learning climate designed to

Re-measuring the learning climate in your organisation		
There is little encouragement to learn new skills and abilities	1 2 3 4 5	People are encouraged to extend themselves and their knowledge.
People are secretive; information is hoarded.	1 2 3 4 5	People share their views and information.
People are ignored and then blamed when things go wrong.	1 2 3 4 5	People are recognised for good work and rewarded for learning.
People are not paid to think; their ideas are not valued.	1 2 3 4 5	Efforts are made to get people to share their ideas.
People do not help each other or share resources.	1 2 3 4 5	People are helpful, pleasure is taken in the success of others.
The higher you score, the more your organisation is likely to be a learning organisation.		

promote motivation and effective performance coaching in your organisation? If you undertake this self–evaluation again it will help you assess the impact of the content of this chapter on your learning.

Further reading

Argyris, C. (1978) 'A leadership dilemma: skilled incompetence', in C. Argyris and D. Schon, *Organisational Learning: A Theory of Action Perspective*. London: Addison- Wesley.

Argyris, C. and Schon, D. (1974) *Theory in Practice: Increasing Professional Effectiveness*. San Francisco, CA: Jossey-Bass.

Boyatzis, R. (1999) 'Self-directed change and learning as a necessary meta-competency for success and effectiveness in the twenty-first century', in R. Sims and J. Veres (eds), *Keys to Employee Success in Coming Decades*. Westport, CT: Quorum Books.

Caldwell, B. and Spinks, J. (1992) *Leading the Self Managing School*. London: Falmer Press.

Cockman, P., Evans, B. and Reynolds, P. (1999) *Consulting for Real People*. Maidenhead: McGraw-Hill.

Covey, S. (1989) *The Seven Habits of Highly Effective People*. New York: Simon and Schuster.

Egan, G. (1993) *Adding Value: A Systematic Guide to Business Driven Management and Leadership*. San Francisco, CA: Jossey-Bass.

Evans, R. (1998) *The Human Side of School Change*. San Francisco, CA: Jossey-Bass.

Garret, B. (1990) *Creating a Learning Organisation*. Hemel Hempstead: Director Books, Fitzwilliam.

Gold, A., Evans, J., Early, P., Halpin, D. and Collarbone, P. (2003) 'Principled principals?', *Educational Management and Administration*, 31(2): 127–38.

Goleman, D. (1998) *Working with Emotional Intelligence*. London: Bloomsbury.

Goleman, D. (2003) *Destructive Emotions and How We Can Overcome Them*. London: Bloomsbury.

Hammer, M. and Champy, J. (1994) *Reengineering the Corporation*. London: Nicholas Brealey.

Nonaka, I. and Takeuchi, H. (1995) *The Knowledge Creating Company: How Japanese Companies Create the Dynamic of Innovation*. New York: Oxford University Press.

Osterman, K. and Kottkamp, R. (1994) 'Rethinking professional development', in N. Bennett, R. Glatter and R. Levacic (eds), *Improving Educational Management*. London: Paul Chapman Publishing.

Parkin, M. (2001) *Coaching and Storytelling*. London: Kogan Page.

Rowan, J. and Taylor, P. (2002) 'Leading the autonomous school', in J. Heywood and P. Taylor (eds), *School Autonomy* European Forum on Educational Administration, Bulletin 2.

Schein, E. (1984) 'Coming to a new awareness of organizational culture', *Sloan Management Review*, 25(2): 3–16.

Senge, P. (1990) *The Fifth Discipline*. London: Nicholas Brealey.

Senge, P., Lucas, T. and Dutton, J. (2000) *Schools that Learn*. London: Nicholas Brealey.

Wellins, R., Byham, W. and Wilson, J. (1991) *Empowered Teams*. San Francisco, CA: Jossey-Bass.

Part II

Theory into practice

This part of the book was written with the following people in mind:

- team leaders, business managers, senior leaders in any walk of life but especially education and other professions; and
- senior leaders, middle managers, practice managers, team members, board members, directors and trustees in education and other professions.

These chapters contain practical case studies drawn mainly from the field of education. In this part of the book I give practical advice on how to put theory into practice.

To be a highly effective leader and coach it is not enough to have good intentions, you also need to have access to tried and tested techniques and processes; the tools of your trade.

From performance management to performance coaching in schools

This chapter is about:

The performance management process used in many schools and how this basic management process can develop into performance coaching if you have the will and the skill to make the adaptation. If you are a teacher, teaching assistant, business manager, team leader, senior leader, headteacher, governor, school improvement officer/partner, adviser, consultant leader or freelance consultant you will benefit from reading this chapter.

I use education to illustrate many of my points as leadership and performance management and coaching in education is my main field of expertise and I expect the main readership of this second part of the book to be associated with education in some sense. For those of you not in education, the material presented can easily be applied to a variety of contexts, professions and businesses. I also use my own organisation as a case study, as it was one of the four organisations used to inform the performance management processes within the English education system. This work is set within the context of the 2006 performance management processes in schools in England, processes that allow performance coaching to take place.

Why is this important?

Performance management is a key process in the self-evaluation of any organisation. Performance coaching takes the process one step further, into improvement. Effective performance management can help you, as team leaders, middle managers, senior staff and governors, 'make a difference' for the adults and students you work with. Performance management processes are excellent if used well but if they are used with a lack of imagination they can become mechanistic and managerial. This chapter takes you through some of the essential elements associated with the often misunderstood management process used in many schools and by all state schools in England. You also need to understand the basic performance management process, how it works and its potential. I cover the basics of performance management as a process but, given the ephemeral nature of the law, there is a 'health warning' about checking the facts are current. To illustrate how the process *can* work, I offer you an exemple of good practice. I take you from performance management to performance coaching.

Self-review

If you are a team leader in a school, or a school leader of any kind (including being a governor) why not have a go at this self-review, which is specifically aimed at you?

Before you read on I would like you to assess your knowledge of performance management in many schools. Towards the end of the chapter I ask you to undertake this first self-review again and assess any changes.

Performance management in schools?	Yes/No
Senior staff agree the school performance management policy.	
The performance management cycle is biannual.	
Team leaders decide whether or not to undertake lesson observation as part of the process.	
Objectives for teachers need only relate to their professional development.	
The governors should not be informed about performance management as it is purely a professional process.	
The answer to all of the above is 'No'.	

In this chapter I offer other self-evaluation opportunities to assess your background knowledge in relation to performance management as often used in schools.

Who does what in performance management in schools?	
1 Keeps teachers' performance review statements secured on file.	
2 Decides on the exact timing of the performance review cycle for teachers.	
3 Ensures that the staff (especially team leaders) are operating as per agreed policy and procedures.	
4 Has responsibility for agreeing the performance management policy and ensuring it is operating effectively.	
5 Ensures that the performance of teachers is reviewed in accordance with the regulations.	
If you answered any of the above incorrectly you may not be using performance management in the same way as many schools. **Answers: Headteacher Q1, Q2, Q3, Governors Q4, Q5.**	

Now check your knowledge of the process of target/objective setting and see if you need to go back to the legislation to clear up any confusion.

Planning and target setting?	Yes/No
1 Regulations and target setting apply to all staff in school, including support/associate staff.	
2 Governors appoint the appraiser (team leader) for teachers and can sit in during the appraisal/review meeting.	
3 Objectives are agreed for the whole appraisal cycle and should not be changed under any circumstances.	
4 Teachers objectives are only related to their pupil development needs.	
5 The teacher has no right to complain about the process if it is not well managed.	
Again if you answered any of the above incorrectly you may not be running performance management in your school in the same way as most others. **All answers = NO.**	

How did you do in these more specific self-reviews? If you need to know a little more or a lot more then read on.

Background

The performance management process used in many schools, especially in England, was first introduced in 2000 by the Department for Education and Employment (DfEE, 2000a; 2000b). The process built on the 'Appraisal' process that was introduced into schools in 1991. In 2006 the Education (School Teacher Performance Management) (England) Regulations 2006 (DfES, 2006) were introduced by what is now the Department for Education and Skills. These regulations built upon earlier regulations and allowed for a more professional and wide-ranging review of the duties of a teacher. The 2006 regulations did not include performance management opportunities for support/associate staff in schools.

Many schools had been using a form of appraisal and/or performance management for many years before the DfEE decided it was a good thing for all schools to adopt. Many schools tended to focus on the professional development and training aspect of appraisal, very few appeared to use performance/management information. The process I introduced into one organisation, in the 1980s, did use lesson/work observation and pupil progress and attainment information to inform the process. The information and data gathered was used to help the senior team analyse the performance of each individual teacher and offer support, training and resources if needed. This early process had an element of coaching but we did not call it that at the time. The support staff soon noticed that the teaching staff valued the process and found it useful. They asked if they could be involved, which was a superb step forward. This process came to the notice of local universities and the DfEE. The process was observed and not approved of, the notion of analysing the performance of individuals was not readily accepted at the time. This was the period when all staff had to be treated the same, no matter how fantastic or ineffective they were – very demotivating for the effective staff and very easy for the less effective staff!

Several years later the DfEE decided the old national appraisal process was not having enough of an impact on children's learning. The old process was good at providing professional development and training but this seemed to lack any observable link to the performance of staff or pupils. Hence the new performance management processes were introduced in England. My organisation was again asked to join in the debate about what the new performance management processes should be like. Worth school was one of four successful organisations the process was based on. The key to the success of the process in our organisation was not the mechanism but the intentions. We set out to help staff understand their strengths and weaknesses, and then help them improve so that their improved skills would help our clients – our pupils – learn more effectively and enjoy their education more. The focus of the coaching and development of the individual member of staff was that the learning of the individual pupil was 'king'. We judged our success by the pupils making good, or better, progress/improvement. We did not focus on attainment or national targets. Although we were happy to call our process performance management, it was in fact a performance coaching process. It took us some time to realise the difference. The 2006 performance management regulations for English schools seek to make performance management a process that holds coaching and professional development at its heart. The 2006 process allows for performance coaching within its framework.

Good practice

I suggested in previous chapters that performance management should be a structured, professional dialogue that reviews and enhances organisational effectiveness, employee motivation and professional development. Even though much of the performance management used in schools is based on a nationally agreed process, it still stands that if it is well used it can be a key tool in moving an organisation on. Moving performance management from being a series of processes and structures to an effective, flexible and focused learning process is at the heart of the development of performance coaching. In the hands of leaders with vision, performance management can help create organisations that have ownership of the process and value its benefits, even though the process was imposed. School and team leaders with vision, courage and understanding should adapt the process within the limits of the law. I helped to create the legislation relating to performance management in English schools and if you read the Act there is a lot of scope for adaptation; less so with the section on performance pay of course. There was, and still is, scope for individual leaders to adapt any national process to the needs of their individual organisation, staff and pupils.

Reading (2003: 17) found teachers, who were using the English performance management processes, commented that:

- They valued a personal professional dialogue.
- 'We can "prove" we have hit our targets.'
- The school is moving in the same direction.
- If the headteacher reveals their school targets it becomes easier for us to shape our classroom targets.
- There is a value in formalising the process, ensuring it happens and having resources/training to support objectives.
- Performance management plugs the gaps.

- Classroom observation has been a boost to morale.
- People are more focused and reflective, and there is more joined-up thinking at school level now.

When they were asked what was still problematic, teachers said:

- The process is still too cosy between some team leaders and teachers.
- There are timetable problems – people leaving their classes to conduct meetings and observations.
- It is difficult getting quality supply cover.
- There are delays in the cycle due to illness, maternity leaves and Ofsted (Office for Standards in Education).
- There is still significant paperwork, which no one will see because the process is largely confidential between the teacher and team leader.
- It is difficult ensuring equity in meeting staff development aspirations.
- Not everyone will get additional financial incentives.
- If performance management is handled badly, staff may feel they are doing a less than adequate job.

Even though this research relates to teacher performance management in England, as it stood at the time, you can learn from the findings to ensure your appraisal/ review meeting is as effective as possible. I use the English process as an example; however, many of the comments made in Reading's research apply to performance management in general. The process was valued if it was managed well (staff feel valued) but there still needs to be a sharper focus on improvement (can be cosy). It is for you as a leader to make this process work for your team. It is for you to turn performance management from a mechanistic process to a valued performance-coaching process that helps your team 'make a difference'.

Legislation for the English school system

The statutory framework (DfEE, 2000b) required that:

- all schools have a performance management policy that is agreed by the Governing Body;
- There is an annual cycle of planning, monitoring and review;
- classroom observations must contribute to the evidence used in setting objectives;
- objectives must relate to pupil progress and professional development;
- roles and responsibilities must be clearly defined; and
- implementation of the policy, and its progress, must be reported to the governing body.

These are the basic requirements of the framework but schools needed to go beyond the basic requirements in order to make the process meaningful in their context. No national legislation or framework will ever be good enough to meet the needs of every organisation in every context. It is for us as school and team leaders to make the process work in our context because we want it to for the sake of our team and pupils. This was recognised and accepted by the government a few years after the national performance management process was introduced.

In his speech entitled, 'School improvement and performance management' (in 2003) David Miliband, Schools Standards Minister at the time, stated:

The prize is that we turn performance management from what many still see as a set of administrative hurdles into an accepted way for school staff to look at their own professional practices and needs. In other words, to turn performance management from a duty into a right.

Miliband went on to point out that his department saw performance management as:

- a way to recognise and promote excellence and professionalism;
- improving the quality of teaching;
- being focused on pupil achievement;
- having the annual appraisal interview as 'just one moment in a continuous process of review and improvement'
- teachers learning from each other on the basis of structured observation and hard evidence;
- identifying professional needs and meeting those needs individually and as part of a team;
- promoting transparent relationships with no hidden agendas and recognising a teacher's right to respond to feedback; and
- reassuring parents and taxpayers that education is idealistic but also hardheaded in promoting high standards.

Miliband describes a process and set of intentions that few would argue with; a process and set of intentions that could be implemented successfully in many contexts beyond teaching. Is your organisation getting close to the ideal Miliband outlines or are you still regarding performance management as an additional burden? Have you thought about adopting the mindset of the performance coach or are you using performance management in a mechanistic way because you are expected to have some form of performance process?

The original framework for performance management in schools (DfEE, 2000b) was not restrictive if read carefully and applied wisely. It built on the original *Education (School Teacher Appraisal) Regulations 1991* (DfEE, 1991) and allowed schools to continue effective practice that was already in place. The basis of the process outlined by Miliband has the potential to be effective if used by leaders who understand the principles of performance management. Such leaders will ensure the process plays a key role in school improvement no matter what national or local initiatives demand. If something is good for pupils and staff, a values–driven leader will ensure that process continues. Such people do not do things because they are required to, but because they believe they work.

Getting started

Make it work in your context

Since 1988, English schools have been offered more autonomy than schools in most other education systems. When I visit schools in other countries I also notice that self-management of schools is becoming more common, autonomy of schools is a rising trend worldwide. The professionalisation of teachers is also a growing trend; in England teaching is regarded as a profession being served by its own professional body. The role of School Business Manager is becoming more accepted in England and that role is also becoming increasingly professional. In many countries the developing autonomy of schools is here to stay, so school and team leaders need the courage to adapt processes to the needs of their context, their staff and their clients (pupils/students).

It may not seem that schools have a lot of autonomy on a day-to-day basis but this is partly down to the fact that many school leaders do not know or test the limits of that autonomy. When I was visiting schools as a ministry adviser or as a consultant, I noticed that few schools actually understood the amount of flexibility that they have. Some school leaders still have the mind-set of an employee; they obey. Schools, professional associations and local government often seem to be inventing their own local rules and limitations to school autonomy. A mythology seems to grow up around any new process that is introduced. Good, professional leaders take hold of new processes and either reject them or make them work for their team, within the law. The best leaders have taken performance management and adapted it, made it work. I suggest the best have turned a national process into a useful coaching process, performance coaching.

Include all your people

Much of the writing in relation to performance management in education, in most countries, only relates to teachers but this does not mean other staff in your organisation cannot be asked or allowed to be involved in the process. If staff other than teachers are to be involved in performance management, a process of negotiation and agreement may need to be gone through. This is actually a sensible and useful thing to do because, if the performance management and performance coaching for all staff is to be valued, they should help shape the process. Many would regard the process of negotiation and agreement to be good practice no matter who is to be involved, whether head-teacher, teacher or support staff, so go ahead and see what your people have to offer. I first introduced appraisal based on performance into a primary school in the 1980s and even then the support staff wanted to be involved as they recognised the process was rational, professional and more about effectiveness and growth than control and blame. If a school is to be fully effective all the key players need to be involved in the performance management/performance-coaching process as they all have a role to play.

Get the culture right

One of the first steps that needs to be taken in ensuring effective performance management and, later, effective performance coaching is to examine the motives, intentions and leadership qualities of those who are to lead and manage it. If the leaders of the process are unclear about why and how the process is to run, what chance is there of motivated but busy staff buying into it? If performance coaching is seen as a bolt-on process, or yet another task designed to take staff away from teaching, then it is destined to fail. All key staff need to be fully behind the process and understand its benefits and limitations. They need to understand their roles and be well versed in them.

So how can you relate all this theory to action in school, what can you do? What might the performance-coaching process be like in practice? In the case study below I outline the broad approach of the school to the national performance management process of 2000.

Case study

The school does not see performance management legislation (DfEE, 2000a; 2000b; DfES, 2006) as restrictive. It believes, if read carefully and applied wisely, these Acts build on the original *Education (School Teacher Appraisal) Regulations 1991* (DfEE, 1991) and allow all schools to continue any effective practice they already have in place.

The school recognises that an effective performance process is a sharp tool in the tool kit of a team leader. It also recognises that in unsound hands the process could be used to control, to ensure uniformity and de-professionalise the team members it is applied to. In the case study school the performance process is used to support, coach and validate good practice whilst respecting and promoting proper autonomy creativity and variety; it is performance coaching. The process is used to support the school's vision and help develop pupils and staff alike; it is an effective instrument in the school but they know any instrument or tool is only as effective as the person who uses it.

(Continued)

(Continued)

The school has a reference to the valuing and development of all staff in the mission statement:

- Encourage each adult member of the school to achieve his/her potential, regardless of age, gender, race or ability.
- Be forward looking, positive and flexible enough to respond to change.
- Support and value all staff and ensure a work–life balance.

Clearly this is only a section of the school mission statement but the fact that three out of a total of eight items relate to staff indicates that the Senior Leadership Team and governors are highly committed to and greatly value staff training and development, and will fund it appropriately. The school believes that receiving and providing high-quality, effective training and development enables the organisation and individuals to continuously improve and develop. Well-trained, well-motivated and effective staff, governors and trainees are a valuable resource which can be used to provide a first-class education for the pupils in our care.

Professional development is linked almost totally to the needs of individual staff, as identified through the performance process. Training has been reduced in quantity but enhanced in terms of quality, impact and monitoring. The school believes effective training and development must impact on the individual member of staff, change behaviour and/or processes, and be seen to impact on pupils.

Objective information and data now informs the appraisal interview, which in turn informs the professional development, coaching and support of individuals and teams. All this informs the development plan. As the skills and capabilities of team leaders became more proficient, the process moved from being a once-a-year event, to being the key process in understanding the organisation, co-ordinating and maximising the talents and aspirations of staff, thereby impacting powerfully on the organisation's climate, culture and results.

What I am illustrating in this case study is that the school did not suffer from the introduction of the legislation relating to performance management. The school adapted the nationally agreed process to the existing positive culture and climate. The leadership team and the team leaders simply took the essentials as laid out in law and set about building on those essentials to create a performance process that was actually for the team leaders and team members in their organisation.

The structure

So what does the performance coaching process look like when it is effective? Here I offer the example of my own school, Worth School, as a case study.

Case study

All staff and governors (board members) are members of one of three teams: the curriculum, personnel (human resource) or resource/finance team. There are no Key Stage or department leaders as the school has a strong primary ethos with policies and methodologies designed to offer smooth progression as the children move from year group to year group. The team leaders understand and accept that one of their key roles is to lead, manage and coach their people, to help them become effective in their task. It is not enough for team leaders to be good at working with pupils; they must also be good at helping their team members grow and develop into effective teachers.

Each team leader is given management time to undertake their roles. All staff/team members are given planning and preparation time to reflect on their work and plan in order to take part in assessment and performance review. This is such a key task that 'quality time' is dedicated to it. In fact, all performance-coaching work is undertaken in quality time provided for the purpose. The process would not work if it were seen as an additional task. The quality time is provided by several part-time members of staff employed on permanent, part-time, contracts. This shows the commitment of the board and senior staff to this process. The school has had a high degree of distributed leadership to all categories of staff, including all types of support staff. The school Business Manager is a team leader and member of the Senior Leadership Team. She undertakes performance reviews with her own team, again all within quality time.

The school has agreed and communicated strategic and operational plans which ensure the curriculum, personnel and resources are focused on enhancing provision for pupils (our clients) and staff. Everybody's part in the process is clear. This focus has made the school more efficient and effective, so staff time, money and resources are not wasted on poor quality or inappropriate resources, training and projects. By being so focused the school has been able to afford cover for staff in order for them to take part in the performance process and be effective as leaders in their various roles and responsibilities.

In this organisation the review and appraisal processes are coherent, integrated and funded as a priority. There are linkages between school development planning, the appraisal meeting, target setting, data analysis, lesson observation and professional development.

This framework for performance carries a health warning: the framework has evolved over many years and is still subject to regular review and adaptation. As staff have been involved in its review and suggested improvements, so the process has improved and staff motivation grown. Staff now own the process at Worth School and the process of ownership tends to be slow, so please do not think that you can simply apply our processes to your context. Start where you already are and build on what is going well. At the same time, slowly reduce or cut out the parts of the process that are not going well. This is kaizen.

The performance-coaching cycle

So what does the performance-coaching cycle look like in any one year? Our cycle has evolved over many years but at the time of writing this book it looked like this.

> ### Case study
>
> All year round:
>
> - 'Quality circle' meetings are held weekly. At these meetings teachers and teaching assistants monitor books and/or pupil work and discuss effective practice and improvement strategies. These meetings are led by subject leaders with their subject coming up for review on a rota basis. Findings are agreed by the meeting, with the subject leader noting improvements needed and ensuring agreed improvements are actioned – a process of kaizen. This is a key part of the school performance coaching process as it offers a form of continuous improvement, an evolutionary process which, if it works well, ensures revolutions are to a minimum!
> - Teachers track all pupils in their class in every aspect of every subject. When a pupil reaches a new stage of performance the teacher records the level against National Curriculum level descriptors (outlined in a later chapter). Staff can also record levels progress and performance on these tracking sheets at the end of a unit of work. These sheets are for teacher use and are not submitted to the team leaders or senior staff unless needed.
> - At several points in the year, every year, work/lesson observations of each member at work in the classroom or in their place of work are made. Team leaders observe the work of the individual under review, record findings and feed those back to the team member. In relation to

(Continued)

teachers this process follows an agreed national process. In relation to other staff it takes the form of a review of work to date. (For example, with the site manager a review of the site and his/her completion of projects will be observed and recorded, the process would review the workload and impact of office staff; with teaching assistants monitoring will be observation of their work with pupils.)

- Coaching, induction and support sessions are organised in relation to the needs of the individual, as identified through the performance process.

Six times a year (half-termly):

- The leadership team focuses on the work of each team in turn and asks the team leader to report the progress made by his/her team. The curriculum team reports on pupil/client progress and improvement (this is outlined below). The personnel team reports on all issues to do with our people, including professional development and deployment of staff to meet the ever changing needs of pupils. The resource/finance team leader (the business manager) report on all aspects of financial and resource application designed to support the work done with pupils and other developments. The main focus of all three teams should be the well-being and development of the pupils in the school.
- The curriculum team reports to the senior leadership Team. The report particularly focuses on the performance of 'target pupils' (pupils who are not performing as well as expected) and is monitored by staff every six weeks (half-termly), with progress and attainment being reported to the school leadership Team at the review of the curriculum team. Resources are focused on areas of poor progress or underattainment, not only those with 'special needs'. This is the regular use of management information to ensure all our pupil/client needs are being dealt with effectively. This rational process of regular analysis of performance and progress data/information is key to the success of performance coaching in the organisation. Team leaders and team members can see that they are being effective, making a difference and having impact. If data shows otherwise, we review our approach for the individual pupil by changing methods or resources. This seems to work for us as it helps us in our key task of providing effective learning for our pupils as individuals.
- The class teachers hold class quality circle debates with their class/group, usually relating to the issues identified by the pupils in the annual audit of pupil opinion. Comments are noted and fed to senior staff who action the points if staff consider them reasonable.

(Continued)

(Continued)

Three times a year (termly):

- The business manager and headteacher meet with the school pupil quality circle to discuss matters of quality of provision in school. Action is taken in relation to agreed action points.
- Teachers make themselves available to parents. Not all parents need to, or do, take the opportunity to meet and review progress. These meeting are held each evening, for one week each term, between 3.30 p.m. and 5.00 p.m. The school does not offer formal parents' evenings.
- Teachers send home a short progress report card, relating to each individual pupil. These are of a tick box format with a few comments offered by the teacher. For the final report teachers send home a full written report, relating to each individual pupil. This is created mainly from a comment bank compiled over a period of years by teachers. These criterion-related comments are supplemented by a closing personal comment by the teacher and headteacher if appropriate.
- The leadership team report progress in relation to a raft of issues, to a full and formal board meeting.
- Team leaders report to the staff and governor members of their team at a full team meeting. They report progress in relation to projects being managed by their particular team.

Once a year:

- Summer: a full audit of individual pupil progress and attainment is undertaken by the class teacher, for every subject. Non-statutory and statutory tests and teacher assessment are used.
- Late summer/early autumn: the full audit data is analysed and reflected upon by class teachers. Progress is compared to targets set in the previous round of appraisal interviews, these targets being informed by previous pupil progress, standardised test information, teacher and team leader professional judgement and negotiation. Next the class data is circulated to all subject leaders, team leaders, senior staff and the special needs co-ordinator. They analyse trends and issues relating to individual pupils, classes and subjects. This helps teachers create a clear picture of pupil progress in the school and what might be done to improve matters. Teachers create draft performance targets relating to each individual pupil in their new class. Subject leaders review their subject, based on the audit data, standardised test data, their own professional judgement and that of the class teachers. Draft class and subject targets are circulated to all team leaders who meet to agree if there are any whole-school issues or individual issues that will need to be highlighted at the appraisal meetings.

(Continued)

- Mid-autumn: national benchmarking data is published and carefully analysed by senior staff. The appraisal meeting takes place, involving class teachers and team leaders. These usually look back at the class and subject result of the last academic year, and agree if other targets had been attained. Next any general points are debated, celebrated or reviewed and recorded. Then the next set of targets are agreed, the draft pupil progress ones being set by the class teacher and usually agreed by the team leaders after some fine-tuning and negotiation. Team leaders hold the legal right to insist on reasonable targets but at Worth this right has never been exercised, as staff (teaching and support staff) tend to set good targets for themselves. The meeting normally lasts an hour with all records being agreed and signed during the meeting.

- Mid-autumn: senior staff gather all data, including benchmark data and so on, and start to turn it into management information which will inform all action plans and the school development plan. The plan for individual, team and whole-school professional development/training is created. Virtually all training and development is based on this plan. The school does not offer ad hoc training; this ensures impact is assessed and staff are not subject to an excess of meetings, on and off site. Subject leaders create draft action plans for their subject(s).

- Mid-autumn: appraisal/performance review meetings are held for everybody who is employed by the organisation. Team leaders lead this process. Target/expectations are agreed, set and recorded for the next year.

- Late autumn: an audit of pupil, parental and staff opinion is undertaken using questionnaires and pupil quality circle discussion information. This soft data and information is vital in helping all team leaders and other senior staff to assess the opinion of the key client of the school.

- Early winter: the review of the content of the opinion surveys of pupils, parents and staff are reviewed and analysed at some length. This part of the review of effectiveness is also key to informing the school development planning process.

- Late winter: a full audit of the facilities and stock is undertaken. All the hard and soft audit and staff review information is used to create the development plan (business/improvement plan). All staff discuss the draft development plan. Later at an open governors meeting called the 'moot' all staff and governors are invited to attend and comment. Governors, of course, have the final word. This meeting takes 90 minutes

(Continued)

(Continued)

as the processes of communication and negotiation have taken place previously with all interested parties. Where possible, finance is allocated on the basis of the action plans and the development plan.

- Late-winter: teaching staff undertake a whole-school 'half-year review' of pupil progress and attainment in English and Mathematics. This process informs the membership of the target groups for the next part year and informs the work of the curriculum team.
- Early spring: the budget is built and plans are actioned. Then the process continues and we return to the start of this cycle.

The cycle we have developed meets our needs at this time. Clearly your context is not the same as ours so you will develop a process or cycle that meets your needs. The process informs our school self-evaluation for inspection and reporting.

Impact on your team?

Reflect on the performance management and performance-coaching processes in your school, ask yourself if they work or not. If it could be more effective then do an analysis of its strengths and weaknesses. Ideally, review this with your team; it need not be a long and complex process, just ask your team how they think the process could be improved in your context. Apply the changes if at all possible, then review again. In this way a bolt-on process becomes owned, valued, sustainable and effective. If your people are very negative you may need to work on culture and climate issues. Make the process, as required by law, your own for the sake of yourself, your team and, most important, your pupils.

Have you adopted a performance process that challenges, coaches and supports individual staff of all types, so they can improve their service to their clients? Is your performance process part of the problem for your staff or part of the solution? As a school leader or as a team leader have you had the will and professionalism to go beyond that which is expected in terms of performance processes and developed a process that really works? If not, why not? An effective performance-coaching process will not only help you move your school forward but also provide high-quality information for self-review.

Impact on you?

So, did you learn anything? Did this rather brief and focused chapter help in any way? Have a second attempt at the self-review you undertook earlier and see if you have improved at all.

Performance management schools?	Yes/No
Senior staff agree the school performance management policy.	
The performance management cycle is biannual.	
Team leaders decide whether or not to undertake lesson observation as part of the process.	
Objectives for teachers need only relate to their professional development.	
The governors should not be informed about performance management as it is purely a professional process.	
The answer to all of the above is 'No'.	

Below is listed some further reading for you.

Further reading

Byham, C. and Cox, J. (1998) *Zapp: The Lightning of Empowerment*. London: Century Business.

Catholic Education Service (2000) *Performance Management in Catholic Schools*. Nottingham: Midland Regional Printers.

Drucker, P. (1986) *The Frontiers of Management*. London: Heinemann.

Handy, C. (1989) *The Age of Unreason*. London: Arrow Business Books.

Johnson, J. (1998) *Who Moved My Cheeses*? New York: G. P. Putnam's Sons.

Lawson, I. (1999) *Leaders for Tomorrow's Society*. London: The Industrial Society.

Mintzberg, H. (1973) *The Nature of Managerial Work*. New York: HarperCollins.

Pedler, M., Burgoyne, J. and Boydell, T. (1991) *The Learning Company: A Strategy for Sustainable Development*. Maidenhead: McGraw-Hill.

Peters, T. and Waterman, R. (1982) *In Search of Excellence*. New York and London: Harper and Row.

Senge, P.M. (1990) *The Fifth Discipline: The Age and Practice of the Learning Organisation*. London: Century Press.

Wellins, R. Byham, C. and Wilson, J. (1991) Empowered Teams. San Francisco, CA: Jossey-Bass.

Performance planning

This chapter is about:

Effective planning and target setting and how these can help you, as team leader, middle manager, senior leader 'make a difference' for your team and the clients you work with. This chapter will take you through some of the essential elements associated with effective planning and target setting. You need to understand the mindset and practice that best promotes these processes and the legal framework that underpins them. Performance coaching still has the need for effective planning as a central process because the coaching needs to result in action and improvement.

Why is this important?

It is important that you do not see planning and target setting as separate, or in addition to, the core function of the organisation, teams or individuals. It is not an isolated function. If your organisation is to develop as a 'learning organisation' it must adopt and use flexible, yet systematic, processes that enable and support continuous improvement through review, reflection, adaptation and planning. The organisational learning that takes place should help align and enhance the capacity of individuals and teams in order to meet the agreed aims, objectives and vision of the organisation. There should be a direct linkage between pupil progress targets, professional development targets, action plans and the school development plan; one should inform the other in a cycle of growth and development.

The processes outlined in this chapter form part of a cycle of planning, monitoring and review. This is a performance process/cycle with interdependent links, each supporting and informing the other. It is perfectly possible to put any of the three stages of the cycle first, as a leader cannot plan until it is clear where the starting point is and one cannot be certain of a starting point without monitoring and review. In the usual tradition we have elected to start with the planning stage in our journey through the performance cycle.

Self-review

Before you read on why not check out your attitude relating to planning and target setting. Please answer the following questions as honestly as possible. Revisit this self-review at the end of the chapter to see if you have changed your view.

Planning and target setting in my organisation:	Yes/Partly/No
Is sufficiently resourced in terms of time, finance and support.	
Aligns the aspirations and objectives of the appraisee with the aspirations and objectives of the organisation.	
Takes account of the constraints on the achievement of appraisee.	
Takes account of appraisee self-review prior to the targets being agreed with an appraiser/team leader.	
Is set in a context of high aspirations, professional respect and development that seeks to assist and coach.	
Check your score: Yes = 2, Partly = 1, No = 0. **How did you get on? The fewer points scored out of 10, the more you need to upgrade your organisation's attitude in relation to effective planning and target setting.**	

Good practice

Planning and target setting need to be clear, manageable, attainable, aligned with the objectives and direction of the organisation, and owned by the team members. At the case study school, for several years the plans, objectives and targets for team and individual professional development and training were not aligned properly with the targets, objectives and direction of the school.

Scenario

John was talking with a well-respected researcher and academic, at a conference dinner, when it occurred to him that several of the effective processes in his school were not at all linked; yet clearly they should have been.

For several years John's organisation had been regarded as well managed and very effective in terms of staff development and support. The organisation was one of the first in the country to get the Investors In People award and had received wide praise for that achievement. The organisation also did well in terms of its work with clients. The researcher, Ros L, was asking John about the organisation where he was leader. John was outlining some of the successes and failures of the organisation when Ros asked him a question that seemed unusual and that he could not answer. She asked him how he knew the training and development of staff in his organisation was effective. John took a deep breath and replied that if staff said it was effective then it must be. Ros was not convinced by this answer. Neither was John if truth be known. It occurred to John that he was always pointing out that clients were his first concern but here he was defending a process that spent money and time on staff with no clear link to enhanced provision for, or satisfaction of, his clients.

It was clear to John and Ros that the money, care, coaching and time spent on staff did have an impact on the pupils but it could not be demonstrated or supported by evidence. What was happening was John had two processes running side by side with no linkage. What linkage there was happened by good fortune, and John was not one to rely solely on good fortune!

When John got back to base he pointed out to his staff that there was no clear link between effective training and development of staff and enhanced provision for, or satisfaction of, their clients. Soon the organisation carried out a detailed study attempting to detect and quantify a direct link between training/professional development and enhanced provision for clients and performance. Within months of quality training and development being put in place, based on an analysis of weakness, clients were reporting that they enjoyed provision more and performance was observed to improve; so had staff confidence.

Now John and his team leaders used audit and review data to inform professional development needs for individuals and teams. Through a detailed analysis of performance data and information, John and his team leaders now expect to see enhanced performance or improved client feedback as a result of carefully targeted professional development and training. There is still a place for training and development of individuals that is about their promotional and motivational needs, but most training and development is now linked directly or indirectly to the core business of the organisation and the needs of the individual team member.

So what John originally had was good intentions, application, effort even applied resources and finance, but much of this valuable human and financial resource was not actually helping his staff perform more effectively.

Encouraging your team members to attend good quality professional development and training events cannot be wrong can it? In fact, even a quality training event can detract to some degree from the effective performance of your organisation and your team members. Good quality team members are a vital asset, and if they are not working with or for the team because they are away learning something they already know, do not need to know or do not want to know how can they contributing to the performance of the team or the organisation? Then, of course, there is the actual cost of the training event, travel, stand-in/temporary staff, goodwill, and physical and mental effort to factor into the calculations, all for little impact on the actual needs of the individual, team and organisation!

Since introducing more focused, targeted and aligned professional development and training the case study organisation has saved time, goodwill, the mental and physical effort of team members and, of course, money. The performance of the organisation continues to improve year on year. If you examine the situation you will find many of your staff expend considerable effort in attending training and development events off-site. This expenditure of effort, goodwill and finances is fine if the event helps them improve in a way they accept, but if the event is not relevant to them or their team they actually become demotivated. If you ask them, many staff will tell you that they object to the driving, map reading, parking, early start, planning and expense expended to no real impact back at base. If the event is relevant and useful then quite the reverse seems to be the case even though the effort and expenditure is identical. One motivates, one does not.

Getting started

The first step that needs to be taken, in ensuring effective target setting and planning, is to ensure there is clarity about every aspect of the process. All involved need to be clear as to the purpose, timings, type and range of targets and objectives set. Protocols need to be set, discussed and agreed by all parties. The role and extent of self-review needs to be taken into account, as do the procedures for disagreement and appeal. If there is clarity, transparency, consistency, honesty, respect and professionalism in the process everyone will understand how it works, why it works, what it works for, what their part is and what to do if disagreement occurs. Quite how all this is discussed, agreed and implemented depends on the climate and culture in your organisation. If there are issues relating to the context then detailed discussion may be needed, with all steps and decisions being recorded and reviewed formally. If the context you find yourself in is more positive and open, agreement still needs to be made, recorded and reviewed but the process can afford to be more flexible, less formal and completed more quickly.

Once the roles are agreed upon you need to decide who is to carry them out; form always follows function. This is the point when specific and targeted training is needed to put in place the necessary skills. There needs to be effective training for target setting and individually planning, operational/action planning and strategic planning. If the process of target setting is to benefit the pupils, the appraisee and the wider organisation, then the process needs to be done with expertise. You cannot be half-hearted about this; if it is important enough to be done, it is important enough to be done professionally. There is no room for the amateur in this process.

Performance and progress expectations

In the case study organisation they tend to use the term 'expectations' for the progress/improvement and attainment/performance targets. The expectations have been worked out over many years of performance and progress analysis. The general school 'expectations' are subject to review and have been agreed by all team members (not only teachers). The progress and performance expectations offer an internal 'benchmark' against which teachers can assess the progress and performance of their pupils. This set of expectations also gives team leaders and team members a benchmark and guide to use for performance management and coaching purposes. If pupils are progressing and performing in line with or above school expectations, then the pupils, teachers and school will be adding value to the education of the individual pupil as assessed by his/her baseline attainment compared with on entry to the school. Finally, the term 'expectations' does not imply this process is soft and over-flexible. Team members suggest their expectations to their team leader, who benchmarks them against school and national expectations/norms. If expectations are not met at the end of the year an in-depth discussion is held relating to the factors that prevented the expectation being met, what the school calls 'other factors'. It has been accepted as motivating for team members (and pupils) to have expectations/targets/objectives/goals, whatever you want to call them. I have found team members like to have a view of their impact, providing that view is humane, logical, professional, attainable and rarely brings blame except when it is clearly due.

Pupil progress and attainment targets

I am going to use our case study school, Worth School, to illustrate detailed target setting for each pupil/client. This example uses education, but again the learning can be applied to the setting of targets or objectives for clients in many professional settings. In the case study school pupil progress and attainment targets are not expressed and recorded in word form but in numerical and letter form. Each teacher undertakes a review of progress made in the previous class, observes his/her children for several weeks to check validity and then sets targets for each child for the forthcoming academic year. The procedure is outlined below. This process was evolved over many years, initially only Mathematics, English and Science targets were set and assessed but now it is quite easy to set targets for all subject areas as needed.

Case study

The case study school has an agreed view of the expected progress and performance of the vast majority of our pupils (clients/customers, if you are not in education). This set of expectations has been accumulated over a period of years, subject to discussion and review. We think we have a reasonable internal measure/benchmark against which to assess performance and progress/improvement. All team members accept that the performance and improvement of our team members (teachers) and clients (pupils) is not linear and regular. Our 'product' (the pupil) is dynamic and subject to sudden change, to say the least! Holding all this in mind all team members, team leaders and board members are generally content with our set of 'expectations,' for performance/attainment and progress/improvement. We sometimes refer to these expectations as 'targets' and they are recorded in numerical form, but we accept that this is a humane process and our clients are not machines that will perform with regularity.

Holding the school expectations in mind, every October each teacher creates and records expectations/targets for each child in his/her class for every subject. The expectations should indicate how each pupil is expected to progress and record what each pupil is likely to attain, as compared with school-agreed expectations for their age as assessed against National Curriculum levels. The expectations should indicate whether each pupil is likely to be above school expectations (AE), in line with school expectations (E) or below school expectations (BE) at the end of the academic year, in terms of progress and attainment. We assess the pupils by means of statutory or non-statutory tests/assessment for Mathematics, English and Science and internal audit/teacher assessment information for foundation subjects.

The number of children recorded as having serious special needs, which may affect their progress and attainment, should be clearly indicated on the class expectation/target sheet. Children with specific learning, behavioural or emotional difficulties will be set expectations but 'other factors' can be taken into account. For all pupils, factors such as severe family unrest, illness and so on are always taken into account.

(Continued)

(Continued)

We also assess the Non-Verbal Reasoning (NVR) Quotient (IQ) of each pupil each year when they reach the age of 7 or above. We find this information useful when discussing the expected attainment and progress of individual pupils. Subject to no negative factors being presented, pupils of well above or above average ability (more than NVRQ 115) would be expected to make progress and attain above school benchmark expectations (AE). Those whose ability is broadly in line with national norms (NVRQ 85–115) would be expected to be in line with school expectations for progress and attainment (E). Those scoring less than NVRQ 85 would be expected to work at or above school expectation but the score on the NVR would be discussed as a factor. It is expected that pupils with no noted and agreed difficulties/other factors should attain and progress a level in line with or above that indicted by ability on NVR. To add value and make a real impact on provision, teachers aim to move children above the ability range as indicated by NVR.

Draft expectations/targets are drawn up by the class teacher and usually these are agreed with the team leaders at the annual review/appraisal meeting held each October. Draft targets are submitted to the team leader for each teacher prior to the appraisal review meeting. These will be checked by the leadership team prior to formal agreement of the expectations. The fact that the teachers do the analysis and target setting themselves is one element of the coaching aspect of this process, as this information is then discussed and eventually agreed with the team leader; the staff member, not the team leader, managed the process.

Only compulsory assessment target information is published, other expectation/target results are collated and used by governors and senior staff to assess school-wide performance in each subject. Specific data that can identify staff or pupils will not be made available to governors or any other body except in extreme circumstances and with prior notice.

Case study examples of expectation/target setting and review sheets

Figure 6.1 is an illustration of the sheet we use in our expectation-setting process. The sheet appears relatively complex but in fact is very quick and easy to use once you get used to it. This is the sheet the teacher uses to set the results of each individual pupil for last year, his/her expectations for the forthcoming year and, at the end of the year, his/her results in terms of performance/attainment and result in terms of pupil progress/improvement. This sheet is for information and communications technology (ICT) in the last class of primary school, Year 6.

WORTH PRIMARY SCHOOL

AUDIT REVIEW AND EXPECTATION SETTING SHEET

SUBJECT: ICT   ACADEMIC YEAR ..... YEAR 6

PUPIL INFORMATION (CONFIDENTIAL)

PREVIOUS ACADEMIC YEAR				PRESENT ACADEMIC YEAR			
PUPIL NAME	NVRQ Test Score Previous	SAT Audit Previous	Expectation Set	NVRQ Test Score Present	SAT Audit Present	Progress Present	BE/E/AE Present
John	121	4A	5B	122	5C	+ 0.3	AE
Jenny	128	4A	5B	119	5B	+ 0.6	AE
Sid	128	4B	5C	122	4A	+ 0.3	E
Alex	91	3B	4A	97	4B	+ 1.0	BE

CLASS INFORMATION   ICT   YEAR 6 YEAR ....

	PREVIOUS ACADEMIC YEAR						PRESENT ACADEMIC YEAR					
	NVRQ %Tesl Score Previous		SAT Audit % Previous		%SAT Audit Expectations Set October		NVRQ %Test Score Present		Sat Audit %Present		*Pupil* Progress % Present	
	RS	%	RS	%	RS	%	RS	%	RS	%	RS	%
AE		%		%		%		%		%		%
E		%		%		%		%		%		%
BE		%		%		%		%		%		%

Figure 6.1   *Example of audit review and expectation/target-setting sheet-RS is Raw Score*

Initially the school used a form of target setting that identified percentages of pupils at particular levels of attainment only in Mathematics, English and Science. This form of target setting was dropped as it did not allow for the identification and monitoring of progress and attainment of individual pupils. This purely number-based form of target setting did not assist staff in the tracking of pupils in their own class, or across the school in their subject, for monitoring or report writing reasons. Finally, and most importantly, staff wanted to track and evidence individual pupil progress and improvement, not just attainment data of particular groups of children. As professionals we were target setting to assist our clients as individuals, not to meet some central government target.

In the example above in Figure 6.1, I have included some fictional expectation data to illustrate how the sheet may be completed at or before the autumn appraisal meeting. I use ICT as an example to stress the fact that the school values pupil progress and attainment in all subjects not just Mathematics, English and Science. The columns are as follows, reading from the left:

- The first column is for the name of each individual pupil in ICT in the Year 6 class.
- The second column records the NVR Quotient from the previous year.
- The third column records the National Curriculum level as assessed at the end of the previous academic year. This enables the team member (the teacher) and the team leader to assess the attainment made by the pupil one year earlier on this one sheet.
- The fourth column contains the expected level for each pupil to attain by the end of the current academic year. All this is set by the teacher but he/she may not actually input the data. We tend to expect two-thirds of a level progress each year for most pupils.

The first few columns are completed at the start of the academic year and constitute the school target-setting process. Usually Mathematics, English and Science form the focus of the performance appraisal/review meeting, but all other subjects have expectations set and these are discussed if need be.

At the end of the academic year the rest of the columns are completed, analysed and discussed at the performance appraisal/review meeting with the team leader.

- The fifth column records the new NVR Quotient. As indicated previously, this gives us another indicator of ability.
- The new National Curriculum levels are added in the sixth column. Those of you in teaching will notice that we record our level five score at three levels, ABC, yet the standard assessment task (SAT)/national test does not, even though they should. We calculate these sub-levels from the actual points the pupils attain on the tests.

- The seventh column shows in decimal form the progress made by the pupil. The school expects most pupils to make 0.66 of a level progress each year. To save time we just record this as 0.6. This is the column that receives the most attention as team leaders and teachers feel very motivated by good pupil progress rather than simple attainment.
- The eighth and final column shows whether or not the pupil is AE, that is, above school expectation, E, that is, in line with expectation or BE, that is, below expectation.

Progress and improvement are the holy grail

As you can see from the fictitious data, John is a bright boy, did well last year and got a good end-of-year attainment result this year, which puts him ahead of school expectations and national expectations. You may think John has done well, but you will notice he has only made 0.3 progress, which is below the school expected progress. This would be a point of discussion for teacher and team leader as progress is the holy grail at the school. Conversely, Alex is not as bright and only attained a moderate level the previous year, but notice that Alex progressed by a whole level, which is the equivalent of two years' work in one year. Even with this superb progress Alex is still below school expectations for most children of his ability. This teacher would be expecting positive comments from his/her team leader as the teacher has ensured superb progress for Alex even though more is needed.

In the second box at the bottom of the expectation sheet data from the individual information in the boxes above is collated and recorded. This is a record of the whole class and allows an overview of class or group progress and attainment for any subject or any aspect of a subject. This could also record the collated data of a year group in a school larger than single form entry. Note that this data is confidential, subject to agreed limitations. The class information boxes give senior staff and subject leaders an overview of their subject results in every class, which is helpful for benchmarking and reporting purposes. With this data the school can asses its performance in any one subject, which is useful for planning and budgeting reasons such as planning team professional development and training.

These two sets of information allow team leaders and senior staff to assess the performance of teachers in terms of teaching individual pupils, subject results in an individual class and subject results for the whole school. We find this to be really useful management information for planning our next steps for individual team members and the organisation as a whole.

Progress and attainment in Reception Year are measured against baseline/achievement-on-entry data, currently called Stepping Stones and Early Learning Goals, which are gathered within six weeks of each child starting in

Reception. Throughout the first year of school pupils are assessed against these descriptors.

Case study written objectives

The case study school uses a cover sheet to record the main details, dates, names, comments, signatures, and so on. This cover sheet also lists the main point of the discussion. Written objectives are then recorded on an 'action sheet' which is commonly used in the school to agree and record most internal action plans. The case study school does not see the point in reinventing or redesigning processes that work well. A second sheet, identical to that in Figure 6.2, is used to record any training and development objectives; the sheet being sent to the personnel team leader so he/she can build all the individual training and development objectives into a training and development action plan which supplements the school strategic plan/development plan.

All this is informed by, and serves to inform, the school's strategic plans, its development plan. This linkage is explored further in the chapter relating to the review meeting as, of course, each part of the process of planning, monitoring and review is set firmly within the context of the development plan and school improvement.

Impact on your team?

Some of the case study examples I have offered are more detailed and technical but I hope you have found them practical and of some use. This process has been observed by many organisations and so far we have found no other process that serves us as well. All this is now recorded and stored electronically by support staff. For some time we have been testing out software to see if we can find a package that does all we want it to, from the tracking of progress and attainment for every child in every subject to whole-school analysis of every subject. This process does require thought and effort, but my teams find it sustainable and useful. I hope you can find some use for the information provided.

As you can see, the target-setting process used in our performance-coaching process is not very different from that used in performance management. There are differences however. In the coaching process the team member does his/her own analysis and target setting with the support of the team leader. The team leader does not lead the process but coaches the team member through it. The team leader can impose targets and plans, but I have never known this to happen in my own organisation. This then results in the plans looking quite normal but the process offers more ownership and engagement for the team member. In this way we find staff are more likely to actually keep plans and targets in mind when working.

OBJECTIVE	HOW	SUCCESS CRITERIA	WHO	WHEN	COST £	DONE [date]

Figure 6.2 *Example of training and development objectives sheet*

Impact on you?

Complete the self-review again and assess any change in your view or learning. What do you think now?

Planning and target setting in my organisation:	Yes/Partly/No
Is sufficiently resourced in terms of time, finance and support.	
Aligns the aspirations and objectives of the appraisee with the aspirations and objectives of the organisation.	
Takes account of the constraints on the achievement of appraisee.	
Takes account of appraisee self-review prior to the targets being agreed with an appraiser/team leader.	
Is set in a context of high aspirations, professional respect and development that seeks to assist and coach.	
Check your score: Yes = 2, Partly = 1, No = 0. **How did you get on? The fewer points scored out of 10, the more you need to upgrade your organisation's attitude in relation to effective planning and target setting.**	

Further reading

Brighouse, T. and Woods, D. (1999) *How to Improve Your School.* London: Routledge.

Cheshire Advisory Service (n.d.) *A Handbook: School Teacher Appraisal.* Chester: Cheshire County Council.

Covey, S. (1989) *The 7 Habits of Highly Effective People.* New York: Simon and Schuster.

Department for Education and Employment (DfEE) (n.d.) *Getting the Most From Your Data.* London: Standards and Effectiveness Unit.

Department for Education and Employment (DfEE) (2000b) *Performance Management in Schools: Performance Management Framework.* DfEE 0051/2000. London: The Stationery Office.

Department for Education and Employment (DfEE) (2000a) *Performance Management in Schools: Model Performance Management Policy.* London: The Stationery Office.

Department for Education and Skills (DfES) (2002) *Embedding Performance Management: Training Modules.* London: DfES.

Fullan, M. (1991) *The New Meaning of Educational Change.* London: Cassell.

Gann, N. (1999) *Targets for Tomorrow's Schools*. London: Falmer Press.

Hammer, M. and Champy, J. (1994) *Re-engineering the Corporation*. London: Nicholas Brealey.

Hargreaves, D. and Hopkins, D. (1991) *The Empowerd School*. London: Cassell.

Pedler, M., Burgoyne, J. and Boydell, T. (1991) *The Learning Company: A Strategy for Sustainable Development*. Maidenhead: McGraw-Hill.

Performance monitoring

This chapter is about:

Effective monitoring and information gathering by means of work/lesson observation, quality assurance, the gathering of (pupil) progress and attainment data, and giving feedback; the gathering of management information data. Most of the suggestions offered in this chapter will be of general use to any profession or business but I will continue to use education as my main focus. My case study materials are drawn from my own organisation, a school. Performance coaching is a process based on evidence and observation, as is good quality sports coaching.

Why is this important?

For monitoring to be effective for coaching, you need to know what its purposes are. You need to know how the monitoring is to be conducted, what information is to be gathered, how it is to be gathered and how it is to be recorded, used and stored, and who is to have access to it. You also need to understand the mindset that best promotes effective monitoring and the performance-coaching framework that underpins it.

Self-review

What is your attitude to monitoring performance? Have a go at this self-review and see how you measure up.

Monitoring:	Yes/Partly/No
Is a way of gathering accurate and objective data and information that underpins the review process.	
Is so vital that those involved need to be trained and practised in the skills needed to monitor effectively.	
Should be seen as being a key tool in helping staff focus on their core task.	
Should be transparent, rational, sustainable and low in bureaucracy.	
Has balanced, objective and developmental feedback built in.	
Score: Yes = 2, Partly = 1, No = 0. **The fewer points scored out of 10, the more you need to reflect on your attitude to monitoring and the giving of feedback.**	

So how did you perform in relation to this self-review? I should think by now you are getting the hang of this process and can answer with a high degree of success.

Good practice

Effective performance coaching and performance motivation, in any profession or business should be based on evidence, and gathered in a rational, ethical, transparent and professional manner. The data gathered is analysed and turned into information, which in turn informs a knowledge base relating to the processes in the organisation. The information and knowledge gathered informs feedback. Effective feedback should be timely, relevant and from a credible source.

A sound knowledge of what is going on in an organisation is a prerequisite to effective planning and action. To plan or act on inaccurate or incomplete data, information and knowledge is not professional and may lead to damage being done to individuals, teams and the wider organisation. It is notoriously difficult to ensure objectivity in the monitoring and review process, especially in relation to human interaction, but it is incumbent upon those involved in performance coaching to attempt to be objective, ethical and professional at all stages of the process. Ineffective organisations and individuals 'plan, do and fire fight'; effective ones 'plan, do, monitor, reflect/review and then adapt'. The monitoring and review process is an essential element in the cycle of continuous improvement. Without effective monitoring and review organisational and personal adaptation and improvement is likely to fail.

Scenario

Sally had been working as an advisory headteacher for some time. She had visited many schools in several areas of her local education authority and reported on the implementation of the new National Curriculum and the associated assessment procedures. Sally was used to visiting schools who were working hard to implement and monitor the new curriculum, however, on this visit she was surprised at what she found.

The school she visited was a large three-form entry, primary school which generally had a sound reputation. During her visit Sally was to meet with the headteacher and then monitor assessment in each of the three Year 2 classes. Upon her arrival Sally was informed that the headteacher was too busy to meet her and Sally was to be taken to monitor each class in turn. In the first classroom Sally met and observed an experienced teacher who was working in a manner she recognised as effective. From the teaching observed and the work scrutinised it appeared the new curriculum was taught well.

In the second classroom Sally met a young teacher who had a philosophy, approach and style which was very different to that of her colleague. Her philosophy may best be described as 'progressive'. The children were allowed to select their work, with a significant number apparently not selecting work associated with reading and writing. The standards of behaviour and work presented appeared poor to Sally, with little actual evidence being available.

In the third room visited there was almost total silence, with little movement of pupils within the room. The teacher asked Sally if she would like to see examples of work, she then proceeded to call one child to her desk and point out, to Sally, in front of the child, that this child's work is an example of poor work!

Sally eventually managed to see the headteacher and report her findings. The final surprise came when Sally found the headteacher did not know what was going on in the school. She did not know three contrasting philosophies and methodologies were being implemented in one year group.

If this school had a process of monitoring and review of teaching and pupils' progress data, the headteacher and senior staff would have known what was happening in each of these three classrooms. More importantly, they would have been able to observe and assess the impact on pupils of each approach and decide which, if any, was the most productive and ethical. To decide on a course of action based on sound research and evidence, many would regard as a professional process, even if they disagree with the conclusions drawn. To allow staff so much freedom, without any assessment of the consequences, indicates a lack of professional accountability, leadership and vision. This is an illustration of a variation between classes and teachers in the same school. We are well aware of variation between schools, but are we sufficiently aware of internal variation and its impact on pupils? This is a question you may like to ask yourself.

Getting started

If monitoring is to be successful, it needs to be set in a positive climate. Here the mindset and attitude of the senior team leaders is vital. If the attitude and mindset of the senior team is not right, it is vital that middle managers and team leaders help them get it right otherwise the process will not be effective. The basis of monitoring, especially lesson observation, needs to be sound and seen as such by staff at all levels. Lesson observation, as with all of the performance process, is a sharp tool in the tool kit of a leader or manager. It is only right that all involved should want to ensure lesson observation and monitoring is used properly to help, not hinder. In unsound hands monitoring can be used to control, to ensure uniformity and to de-professionalise. In sound hands monitoring can be used to support, coach and validate good practice whilst respecting and promoting proper autonomy and variety. Used with flair, the process can be used to support the school's vision. It is a sharp instrument but it is only as effective as the person who uses it! The reason why monitoring is seen as unpopular or ineffective in some schools is not down to the process but the skills and intentions of those who use it.

It cannot be stressed too much that, like the target-setting and review processes, monitoring needs to be discussed by all involved in an attempt to create clarity relating to the protocols needed. You need to answer the questions relating to the number of lesson observations to be conducted by team leaders. Will they observe once, twice or three times per year? What happens to observations undertaken by subject leaders and senior staff as part of their routine monitoring? Will this form part of performance monitoring on every occasion, only if relevant, only if agreed or only if what is observed is significant? Recent legislation is clearer about these questions but leaves them open for each organisation to agree in a professional manner. Further questions will be asked relating to practical matters such as what does the observer do if a child is hurting another but the teacher has not seen this? Does the observer intervene and risk spoiling the observation or does the professional duty to protect the child come before a fly-on-the-wall approach to observation? It may be that your people want the observer to sit in an agreed place in the room and stay there. It maybe that you all agree to become involved and enjoy interaction with groups or individuals. All this depends on the climate in your organisation and possibly the age and ability of the pupils. What is acceptable in a sixth form college may not be in a Reception classroom or a special needs unit. The important thing is that there is clarity and that the process is effective and reviewed regularly.

The process

The process used in many schools requires team leaders to undertake:

- monitoring of a teacher's performance against his/her agreed objectives; and
- observing his/her teaching at least once during the review cycle.

This aspect of traditional performance management is just as useful in performance coaching. The person undertaking the monitoring of the lesson(s), review of pupil data and other material must consult the reviewee before obtaining oral or written information from others relating to performance of the reviewee. Monitoring should be regarded as a process not an event.

Training materials linked to the national framework for performance management in England (DfES, 2002) suggest that (I paraphrase) all of the monitoring activities that take place in a school contribute to the collection of evidence for performance review. The training material suggests that effective monitoring means paying continuous attention to progress (towards the agreed objectives and development) during the year. Monitoring is the process of finding out by observation, discussion, reading, listening, analysis, what is actually happening and judging the impact of the activities. In the business world, monitoring is often referred to as 'quality assurance', in other words, having agreed what should happen (objectives), are we doing what we agreed and do we need to make any adjustments or changes?

In addition to the monitoring of teaching by lesson observation and pupil progress records, other items and processes can be monitored, such as written plans, pupil records, responses to continuing professional development/training, curriculum leader's monitoring of subjects, tests/examination results, and pupils' written, oral and creative work.

Lesson observation

The training of team leaders is vital, they not only need to understand the process but have practised the skills needed. It is vital that they are trained in lesson observation by a colleague who is experienced in how to behave, what to look for, how to moderate judgements and how to give feedback. This is no easy task. The same (DfES, 2002) training materials suggest the very least team leaders need to be able to do is to:

- recognise achievement;
- judge progress towards achievement of objectives;
- identify areas where further support is needed;
- keep initiatives on track;
- identify need for change of direction (amend objectives, for instance);
- identify further professional needs of teacher;
- judge consistency and quality; and
- judge impact of activities on school/standards.

Lesson observation needs to be planned and systematic, not incidental and generalised. It needs to be focused on the activities needed for progress towards achievement of objectives. It should not only monitor progress towards objectives but also be part of the coaching support for teachers. In this way the process may be seen as a positive activity performed by colleagues whose main goal is to ensure the best provision for their pupils. The training material goes on to suggest (DfES, 2002) that team leaders must seek to avoid:

- un-preparedness for a lesson observation visit;
- lack of clarity about what is to be monitored;
- inconsistency in monitoring activity;
- lack of focus;
- lack of feedback;
- feedback badly handled; and
- no feedback on impact of activity only description of what happened.

These are reasonable coaching points for the team leader. If the team leader is to be respected as a coach by team members then he/she needs to lead by example.

There is no single format for recording lesson observation, however, this process must be as objective as possible. If you are to do lesson observations you would be well advised to log events clearly and note the timings, behaviours, language used, and so on. When you feed back that a teacher observed missed a request for help from a pupil whilst dealing with children who walk out or call out, you need evidence of who waited and was ignored, and for how long. You also need to note the children who ignored the instructions of the teacher, again noting who, how often and in what way. This might sound clinical but some teachers are not aware of their own behaviours and how these can encourage and reward the poor behaviour they do not want. This level of evidence gathering takes practice. Clearly, evidence gathering should have a focus, usually on an agreed activity. However, if an issue presents itself it should not be ignored. A good balance of positive and developmental points should be noted.

Pupil progress and achievement data

The monitoring of pupil progress and attainment can be carried out in many ways. Again there is no single best way to do this task. Every individual and school context is different. In the previous chapter, we offered examples of good practice in the recording of progress expectations/targets in data form. You need to be sure that everyone is clear as to what evidence is to be gathered, in what way and how often.

Case study school: agreement on the use of data for monitoring

The leadership team and/or subject leaders may wish to gather data in elements of Mathematics, English and Science not included in the non-statutory and statutory assessment, and for foundation subjects. The data from this type of audit is not essential for statutory assessment or expectation/target-setting reasons but may be deemed useful by the leadership team or subject leaders. Such auditing methods will be designed according to our needs, by the subject leaders, in consultation with the curriculum team leader. This data is solely for the purpose of internal performance management and should not be taken into account for analysis of statutory assessment scores.

Data from statutory assessment will be gathered and recorded as prescribed by law. Such data will, if possible, be transcribed in order to be of use to the school for analysis and performance coaching purposes. All audit data (statutory and non-statutory) is to be put into class-based batches and used by the present /future teacher for analysis.

Copies of all data should be submitted to the subject leaders, leadership team and the school special needs co-ordinator (SENCO). Teachers, subject leaders and the SENCO should gather and analyse this data before their appraisals, when the data will be reviewed and new targets agreed. Data will inform of problems in the system and give evidence for development. In relation to the uses of pupil progress and attainment data for expectation/target setting and review, a policy of no blame will be followed in the case of reasonable and professional effort by the staff involved.

In addition to the above, books will be scrutinised regularly for much of the year. Subject leaders will monitor the work produced in their subject on a rota basis. A weekly 'quality circle' meeting will be held where the books from each subject are scrutinised, with action and improvement being based on the evidence drawn from the work of the pupils. The school will focus on input and outcomes rather than process. Maximum freedom will be offered to class teachers and other staff in terms of methodology and processes.

(Continued)

(Continued)

All classroom staff will attend the quality circle meetings related to learning. All staff will attend quality circle meetings linked to wider school issues and procedures. All classroom staff will be involved in the monitoring of pupil attainment and progress, guided by the relevant subject leader. The subject leader will note the main findings and action any developments.

The case study school is attempting to focus its attention more on what the pupils are learning and the supporting evidence, rather than teaching; this is a focus on outcomes based on sound objectives and expectations. The school has very few other 'staff meetings' beyond planned professional development/training, quality circle meetings and occasional briefing meetings. The team leaders and senior staff do not monitor teaching plans or require teachers to plan jointly. This is a radical shift from the monitoring of input, or alleged input, to actual outcomes. The school believes learning is more important than teaching and planning. This radical policy works well with experienced and effective staff. Of course, all inexperienced staff have plans monitored by mentors or senior staff. You may buy into this logic you may not; what is important is you make the process work in your context.

Feedback and coaching

There is no single, correct time or method for giving feedback to a member of staff who has been observed. This is down to the judgement of the observer and his/her awareness of the colleague who has been observed. It is advisable to ask when it would be best to hold the feedback meeting. The meeting should be a dialogue and form part of the coaching and development of the teacher observed. Key points should be recorded for use at appraisal. Poor performance should be noted and support and advice offered. Negative feedback is best offered as part of a balanced feedback, as many teachers have to go back into the classroom after feedback, so sensitivity is needed. If very poor or unprofessional performance is noted, action should be taken immediately and in line with agreed protocol. Feedback that generates a professional self-evaluation is the most helpful. If you ask a teacher how he/she thought a lesson progressed, you will find the best are reflective and often harder on themselves than you would ever be. With less experienced, reflective or effective staff you may need to be directive, using evidence and instruction to help ensure they progress. This directive method should be used sparingly, as coercive action nearly always bring an equal and opposite reaction in the recipient.

Impact on your team?

Reflect on the information offered in this chapter and think how some of this might be of use in your role in your organisation. My case study examples are linked most closely to teaching, but you may be able to apply the logic in your office if you are a business manager or practice manager. No matter what your role or occupation, the notion of effective monitoring of your essential outcome or performance measure is the same. Set out to do something that is valued, do it, monitor progress and performance and review the process, then start again from the new improved position. This motivates my teams so I hope it will help motivate yours. I find team members like reasonable targets, they do not mind rational and humane monitoring and they like to evidence effective performance and progress.

Impact on you?

Did you learn much during your reading of this chapter; did you change in terms of any of your views? Re-do the self-evaluation and see what impact this has had on you.

Monitoring:	Yes/Partly/No
Is a way of gathering accurate and objective data and information that underpins the review process.	
Is so vital that those involved need to be trained and practised in the skills needed to monitor effectively.	
Should be seen as being a key tool in helping staff focus on their core task.	
Should be transparent, rational, sustainable and low in bureaucracy.	
Has balanced, objective and developmental feedback built in.	
Score: Yes = 2, Partly = 1, No = 0. **The fewer points scored out of 10, the more you need to reflect on your attitude to monitoring and the giving of feedback.**	

If you need to read up on any of this or just find the subject interesting, please do have a look at the further reading list.

Further reading

Department for Education and Employment (DfEE) (2000a), *Performance Management in Schools: Model Performance Management Policy*. London: The Stationery Office.

Department for Education and Employment (DfEE) (2000b), *Performance Management in Schools: Performance Management Framework*. DfEE 0051/2000. London: The Stationery Office.

Esp, D. and Saran, R. (1995) *Effective Governors for Effective Schools*. London: Pitman.

Fullan, M. (1993) *Change Forces*. London: Falmer Press.

Mortimer, P., Sammons, P., Stoll, L., Louis, D. and Ecob, R. (1998) *School Matters*. Wells: Open Books.

Rutter, M., Maughan, B., Mortimore, P. and Quston, J. (1979) *Fifteen Thousand Hours: Secondary Schools and Their Effects on Children*. London: Open Books.

Southworth, G. and Conner, C. (1999) *Managing Improving Primary Schools*. London: Falmer Press.

Performance review

This chapter is about:

How to conduct a performance review, commonly known as an appraisal meeting, and how this links to action planning and strategic planning. The review meeting in performance coaching is more of a structured professional dialogue than a hard-nosed meeting designed to judge outcomes and set targets. Performance is assessed and targets are agreed but the process is driven by the team member, not the team leader.

Why is this important?

As I have suggested in other chapters, the ancient Chinese proverb tells us that 'a journey of a thousand miles begins with a single step', the journey towards your goals and vision begins with a single step, the trick is to ensure that step is taken in the right direction! The right direction for your team might best be discussed with individuals at the review meeting. Get the meeting right and the steps of the individual will probably also be in the right direction; get it wrong and the team member could go backwards in terms of motivation and performance. This is the meeting, above all, where your coaching skills, intelligence, emotional intelligence, common sense and compassion will be called upon, so you need to make sure you get it right.

Self-review

Check if you, as team leader are getting some of the basics right in relation to the review meeting.

Before your next review meeting with one of your team will you have:	Yes	Partly	No
Agreed the date, venue and length of the meeting?			
Clearly established the focus and purpose of the meeting?			
Made sure all parties are clear about their roles and responsibilities?			
Agreed a venue that is comfortable and set out in an appropriate manner?			
Ensured all phone calls are diverted or taken by an answer machine?			
Ensured a method of stopping others from entering the room or knocking on the door?			
Understood that this is a two-way process with both parties fully engaged?			
Agreed a school policy on confidentiality, who is to have access to any documentation and why?			
Agreed note-taking procedures and what will happen to the notes after the meeting?			
Analysed any target setting, self-review and monitoring materials?			
Ensured both parties are notified about any issues that might impact on the meeting?			
Agreed on a moderation process to ensure all involved have equal opportunity?			
Agreed who is to be sent copies of development objectives and agreed a recording format?			

There is a lot to think about here but this is a key meeting and you cannot afford to start it in the wrong setting or context, so these are the sort of practical matters that need a Yes answer. The attitude may be positive but the appraisal will go wrong if you are being interrupted, are too hot, too cold or there is doubt as to the process and its purpose.

Good practice

By now your organisation has ensured all people have individual targets and objectives (expectations) that assist them in their core function, be that ensuring effective learning for pupils in their classes or effective performance of your team members in their office or support roles. Ask yourself, do the individual objectives, expectations and targets, agreed with each team member, fit within the context of the school or organisation and its broader aims? Your team have been monitored and offered support, coaching and professional development, so now we come to the review and appraisal stage, the final stage of one cycle and the foundation of the next. Clearly, if the planning, target and objective setting of the next cycle is to be a 'step in the right direction' you must ensure the review of the previous stage is accurate and provides good enough information to ensure lessons have been learned and progress made.

Ask yourself if the review and appraisal processes in your organisation are coherent and integrated or fragmented with weak linkages between school/organisational development planning, the appraisal meeting, target setting, data analysis, lesson/work observation and professional development. For your processes to be effective it will need to hold the gathering and analysis of progress and performance information and lesson/work observation at its heart. Reflection on objective data forms the basis of good management information, which in turn forms the basis of knowledge relating to the organisation and the individuals within it. Some would say wisdom is difficult to develop without knowledge and information. Quality data, information and knowledge underpin and inform the appraisal interview, which in turn informs professional development, coaching and support of individuals and teams. The cycle of planning, monitoring and review informs the development plan and various action plans, and is the basis of an integrated performance coaching process.

A coaching process, not an event

As you become more proficient the review will move from being a once-a-year event to being the key performance process in understanding the organisation, co-ordinating and maximising the talents and aspirations of staff, and impacting powerfully on the organisation's climate, culture and results. Good team leaders understand the need to ensure goals and objectives are clear and that roles, processes and relationships are effective in helping the appraisee make progress towards the agreed goals. At first you may think it is enough to focus on relationships and structures, and think that changing and improving these will motivate the appraisee. An effective team leader, middle manager or senior manager knows people like to be part of a successful team or organisation and that restructuring or being affiliative is not enough in the long term. A leader at any level, needs to be clear about the goals of the organisation and how relationships and structures are enhanced and aligned in order to meet the goals. In the final analysis you have to recognise that the managing of relationships, structures and processes is done for a purpose.

Getting started

In the case study school the performance coach/team leader should:

- meet with each of the teachers for whom he/she will be the reviewer, before or at the start of the performance review cycle, to plan and prepare for performance review;
- ask if any issues need discussing before the meeting;
- ask for any self-review materials and draft objectives;
- record objectives in writing and allow the job holder to add written comments if he/she wishes;
- monitor performance against these objectives throughout the year, and observe the teacher teaching in the classroom at least once during the review cycle;
- consult the reviewee before obtaining oral or written information from others relating to the teacher's performance;
- meet with the teacher at the end of the performance review cycle to review performance and identify professional development needs/activities;
- write a performance review statement, give a copy to the reviewee within an agreed (or set) number of days of the final performance review meeting, and allow an agreed (or set) number of days for the job holder to add written comments;
- pass the completed performance review statement to the headteacher; and
- pass any record of training or development needs to the organiser of training and development.

The job holder (school teachers who are not headteachers) should:

- play an active role in self-review;
- before the meeting, have a view of targets and objectives he/she needs and pass these to the team leader;
- meet with his/her team leader before or at the start of the performance review cycle to discuss the review arrangements, dates, issues, and so on;
- either agree objectives with the team leader or add written comments to the objectives recorded by the team leader;

- meet with his/her team leader at the end of the performance review cycle to review performance and identify achievements, including assessment of achievement against objectives, and to discuss and identify professional development needs/activities; and
- regard the process as developmental, with self-review and self-improvement as key.

Is everyone in your organisation well trained in the effective use of review and the appraisal meeting? Have team leaders been trained in how to conduct an appraisal meeting? Have they the skills of managing time, active listening, accurate note-taking, questioning (using closed, open and reflective questions), empathy, paraphrasing, challenging and summarising? Conducting an effective review during an appraisal meeting is a complex task that demands skill and appropriate training. If you or your people are not trained and practised at conducting appraisal and review meetings, get this sorted out straight away; this is a sharp instrument and needs to be used with care and by experts, as the potential for damage is high.

A further question you might want to ask is do your people want to hold one or two meetings in the review process? Will one meeting serve as a review of the previous year, a discussion of current issues and allow target/objective setting? There is no right or wrong answer to this question; some organisations favour having two meeting, one for review and one for target setting. Other organisations find one meeting can serve all three stages of the process. A single meeting can act as a link between two cycles, ending one in review and starting the next by agreeing targets and objectives.

Case study school

In the case study school, data-based targets and expectations are set and reviewed on individual sheets that are usually completed, in draft form by the appraisee, before the meeting. Written objectives are recorded on action plans and self-reviewed, in draft, prior to the meeting. This process of self-review speeds the meeting up considerably and usually means it can be completed in less than 90 minutes. Self-review also gives staff a good degree of ownership of the process, and ensures they have reflected on their practice and considered its impact on pupils. It is good practice for an experienced appraiser to let the appraisee talk for a large part of the meeting. The appraiser can act as a coach if the appraisee is engaged in effective self-review. An experienced appraiser, in the role of coach, would

(Continued)

(Continued)

recognise at least three stages in the meeting. The first is that of letting the appraisee tell the story of the year and their progress towards their targets and objectives. In this first phase the appraisee observes, listens and senses, noting key points and emotions. In the second stage the appraiser will prompt, reflect, challenge and draw out alternatives. This is a key phase and needs to be handled differently for each individual. The final stage is that of agreement, recording targets, objectives and development implementation of plans and monitoring processes. A more directive approach will be needed with staff who cannot or will not engage in professional self-review.

Review documentation

I find it useful to have a single sheet on which to record the main points of the review section of the appraisal meeting. During the appraisal meeting a discussion is held regarding the data-based targets and the written objectives. It is usually clear, from pre-meeting documentation and monitoring, if suitable progress has been made. The meeting results in an agreement and recording of what is already known by both parties. It is not good practice to shock people with new evidence at the meeting. The school uses the DfEE (2000c) format for recording the main bullet points. Figure 8.1 is an example of the front sheets used at the school. The sheet is A4 size with other sheets attached as needed. This sheet is completed during the meeting, in handwritten form, with both parties signing it as a correct record at the end of the meeting.

There is space for the appraisee to record a comment; however, the appraiser is not bound by the comment. It is as simple as it looks! The sheet is not typed up or made 'beautiful' in any way. It is simple but effective. I find keeping these records simple and easy to complete means the team leaders can focus on coaching and discussing issues with the team members. The paperwork is often in note form.

Target setting and review sheets – examples of previous versions

The first example of target setting and review sheet (Figure 8.2) used at the case study school, is now over 10 years old. The school has adapted the sheet and improved the process since it was used. I included this sheet as you may find it of some use and it shows the process of continuous improvement in action.

Review record

Name:_____ Job Title:_____

Review Statement

Overall assessment of performance, including achievement of individual objectives
(summarising relevant information)

Statement agreed by: (signature and date)

Post holder:_____ Date: _____/_____/_____

Post holder comments:

Team leader: _____ Date _____/_____/_____

Figure 8.1 *Review document front sheet*

Figure 8.2 identifies the targets and results for all core subjects, an average
of foundation subjects and progress in the subject the appraisee leads at
whole-school level. This sheet does not allow for the identification and monitoring of progress and attainment of individual pupils, which is the price to
pay for simplicity. We have included some fictional outcome data to illustrate
how the sheet may be completed at, or before, the appraisal meeting. In this
particular class each child counts for 3 per cent of the class, in the whole-
school section each child counts for 0.49 per cent of the school. In the case
of AS in Figure 8.2, you can see that there has been good progress in the
teaching of English in this person's class but the subject they lead has reduced
in its effectiveness. The question for you is, are all the sections on this sheet

YEAR GROUP.........ACADEMIC YEAR.........TEACHER.........
NO. OF PUPILS IN CLASS.........%/PUPIL.........

English	Own class	Target set October	Result May	Difference -/+
AS	7 pupils (7 @ 115 VRQ)	= 7 @ 3% = 21 %	9@ 3%=27%	+6%
S	21	= 21 @ 3% =63	21 @ 3%=63	0%
BS	5 pupils (3 SEN + 1 emotional + 1 @75 VRQ)	= 5 @ 3% = 15	3 @3%=9%	-6%
Maths				
AS				
S				
BS				
Science				
AS				
S				
BS				

YEAR GROUP......ACADEMIC YEAR........TEACHER.............

NO. OF PUPILS IN CLASS.............%/PUPIL.............

Foundation Subjects	Own class	Target set October	Result May	Difference -/+
AS				
S				
BS				

Own Subject	Whole school	Target set October	Result May	Difference -/+
AS	60 pupils (@115 + IQ/MQ/VRQ)	60 x 0.43 = 25.8%	55 @ 0.43 = 23.65	-2.15
S	156	156 x 0.43 = 67.08%	156 @ 0.43 = 67.08%	0
BS	14 pupils (6 SEN 3–5 & 5 gen. Low IQ/MQ/VRQ & 1 family stress & 2 new).	14 x 0.43 = 6.02%	19 @ 0.43 = 8.17%	+2.15

Figure 8.2 *Previous target setting and review sheet: example 1*

part of the target set, or only certain aspects. If the target relates to the subject leader role then you have some analysis to undertake and discussion of factors beyond the teacher's control to reflect on.

From the sheet in Figure 8.2 evolved the second example (Figure 8.3), an improved version of the 'class' target setting and review sheet. On this version you can identify individual children with one sheet per subject to be analysed. I have added some fictitious target data. As you can see, the teacher is aiming to move the child up to a complete level in one year; normally children progress at a level every two years. There are only 10 pupil spaces in the example; this would normally be extended to cover a whole class. You can see how James has progressed towards his target and compare this to the most recent standardised test for benchmarking purposes. James is still in the average (inter-quartiles) for ability so you may expect him to score at a National Curriculum level in line with national standards, as he did in Year 4 where the standard is lower level three (3L). In Year 5 the teacher managed to get James to attain at level four lower (4L) which is above the standard expected for this age group. At this time the school did not use the third of levels now commonly used in National Curriculum levelling and tracking. This target is beyond a simple forecast and is aspirational, more than might be expected. This now bring James into a category above standard for his age. Do not aim to move many children up in this way in one year. If each teacher adds a little value year on year, this is how you can make an impact as a team.

In this third example (Figure 8.4) you can see that it is possible to collate the individual pupil results as a whole class and compare it to benchmark data. In this year group you can see that only one child is very bright at 130+ IQ and if you were to 'forecast' you would only expect one child to score at well above standard (WAS). When it comes to target setting the teacher has set a target of 47 per cent as the 130+ child left the school. The result is incredibly good as the group still attain (WAS) at 50 per cent. If this was a Year 6 class that would mean 50 per cent at level 5 which is a whole level above standard for that age. This gives the class an estimated benchmark score of A for that level.

In this fourth example (Figure 8.5) you can see that the collated class or year group data can be further collated and analysed to give an overview of subject in every year class or year group. This gives those with access to this data a very clear view of standards and progress in every class or year group. In Year 2 in this example you will note a huge jump in the number of pupils well above standard. They have been taken mostly from the above standard group. The standard group has risen and the below standard group has reduced in size. There is one child who may be expected to score well below standard on a forecast but he/she has not done so and is probably in the category above.

In the last example (Figure 8.6) the year group/class material is collated into whole-school data for each subject, allowing a clear overview of each

AUDIT REVIEW AND TARGET SETTING SHEET – CLASS

SUBJECT................ CLASS................ DATE................

PUPIL INFORMATION (CONFIDENTIAL)

	PREVIOUS ACADEMIC YEAR 2001/2		2002	PRESENT ACADEMIC YEAR 2002/3			
Pupil name	Eq Mq Nvrq test score previous	Sat audit previous	Target set October	Eq Mq Nvrq test score present	Sat audit present	Progress present	Was, As, S, Bs, Wbs present
James Dean	110	3L	4L	112	4L	1 level	AS

Figure 8.3 *Previous target setting and review sheet: example 2*

CLASS INFORMATION (CONFIDENTIAL)

| | PREV. AC. YEAR 2001/02 | | OCT. 2002 | | PRES. AC. YEAR 2002/3 | | | |
	% Eq Mq Nvrq test score previous	% Sat audit previous	% Sat audit targest set October	0–8% FSM Benchmark target set October	% Eq Mq Nvrq test score present	% Sat audit present	% Pupil progress present	0–8%FSM Benchmark present
WAS	3%	50%	47%	B	0%	50%	0%	A
AS								
S								
BS								
WBS								

Figure 8.4 *Previous target setting and review sheet: example 3*

YEAR GROUP INFORMATION (CONFIDENTIAL........................

DATE..................

		PREV. AC. YEAR 2001/02		OCT. 2002		PRES. AC. YEAR 2002/3			
		% Eq Mq Nvrq Test score Previous	% Sat audit Previous	% Sat audit Target set October	0–8% FSM Benchmark Target set October	% Eq Mq Nvrq Test score Present	% Sat audit Present	% Pupil Progress present	0–8% FSM Benchmark present
R	WAS								
	AS								
	S								
	BS								
	WBS								

Years 1 to 6 Only

		% Eq Mq Nvrq Test score Previous	% Sat audit Previous	% Sat audit Target set October	0–8% FSM Benchmark Target set October	% Eq Mq Nvrq Test score Present	% Sat audit Present	% Pupil Progress present	0–8% FSM Benchmark present
Y1	WAS	0%	17%	53%	A				
	AS	10%	55%	0%					
	S	76%	7%	40%	B/C				
	BS	11%	21%	7%					
	WBS	3%	0%	0%					
Y2	WAS					0%	58%	+41%	A
	AS					43%	3%	–52%	
	S					50%	32%	+25%	C
	BS					7%	7%	–14%	
	WBS					0%	0%	0%	

Figure 8.5 *Previous target setting and review sheet: example 4*

Y1 TO Y6 (NOT RECEPTION) INFORMATION PROVIDED FOR GOVERNORS

PREV. AC. YEAR 2001/02			OCT. 2002		PRES. AC. YEAR 2002/3			
Y1-Y6	% Eq Mq Nvrq Test score Previous	% Sat audit Previous	% Sat audit Target set October	0–8% FSM Benchmark Target set October	% Eq Mq Nvrq Test score Present	% Sat audit present	% Pupil progress present	0–8% FSM Benchmark present
WAS								
AS	15%	17%	20%		17%	22%	5%	
S								
BS								
WBS								

Figure 8.6 Previous target setting and review sheet: example 5

subject. The data can be compared to benchmarking materials and data relating to other subjects, allowing comparison and analysis of differences, strengths and weaknesses. This is completed in the same way as the fourth example but with whole-school numbers for each subject, not class numbers.

Current expectation/target review sheets

You first saw this example (Figure 8.7) of our current expectation and review sheet in Chapter 6 about planning target and expectation setting. In this chapter I focus on the review element of the document, as the same document is used for both target/expectation setting and target/expectation review. Again we find this simple and easy, saving time and effort. You may prefer the earlier versions of this document for use in your organisation.

As you will recall, in the example I have included some fictional expectation data to illustrate how the sheet may be completed at or before the autumn appraisal meeting. I use ICT as an example to stress that the school values pupil progress and attainment in all subjects, not just in Mathematics, English and Science.

Reading the first audit sheet, from left to right:

- The fourth column is the column that contains the expectations/targets as agreed by the team leader at the previous review meeting held with the teacher the previous October.
- The fifth column records the new NVR. As indicated earlier, this gives us another indicator of ability.
- The sixth column contains the new national curriculum levels. Those of you in teaching will notice that we record our level five score in third levels ABC, yet the SAT/national test do not, even though they should. We calculate these sub-levels from the actual points the pupils attain on the tests.
- The seventh column shows in decimal form the progress made by the pupil. The school expects most pupils to make 0.66 of a level progress each year. To save time we just record this as 0.6. This is the column that receives the most attention as team leaders and teachers feel very motivated by good pupil progress rather than simple attainment.
- The eighth and last column show whether or not the pupil is AE, above school expectation, E, in line with expectation or BE, below expectation.

You will recall that the first few columns are completed at the start of the academic year and constitute the school expectation/target setting process. Usually Mathematics, English and Science form the focus of the performance appraisal/review meeting, but all other subject have expectations set and these are discussed if need be.

WORTH PRIMARY SCHOOL

AUDIT REVIEW AND EXPECTATION SHEET

SUBJECT: ICT   YEAR 6

ACADEMIC YEAR

PUPIL INFORMATION (CONFIDENTIAL)

PUPIL NAME	PREVIOUS ACADEMIC YEAR			PRESENT ACADEMIC YEAR				
	NVRQ Test score Previous	SAT Audit Previous	Expectation set	NVRQ Test score Present	SAT Audit Present	Progress Present	BE/E/AE Present	
John	121	4A	5B	122	5C	+0.3	AE	
Jenny	128	4A	5B	119	5B	+0.6	AE	
Sid	128	4B	5C	122	4A	+0.3	E	
Alex	91	3B	4A	97	4B	+1.0	BE	

CLASS INFORMATION

ICT

YEAR 6   YEAR 2005/2006

	PREVIOUS ACADEMIC YEAR				PRESENT ACADEMIC YEAR							
	NVRQ % Test Score Previous		SAT Audit % Previous		% SAT Audit Expectation Set October		NVRQ % Test Score Present		Sat Audit % Present		*Pupil* Progress % Present	
	RS	%	RS	%	RS	%	RS	%	RS	%	RS	%
AE												
E		%		%		%		%		%		%
BE		%		%		%		%		%		%

Figure 8.7 *Current target setting and review sheet*

The review/appraisal interview between team member and team leader takes place in October and the first third of the meeting is taken up with a review of the team members' results in terms of progress and attainment performance. The last four columns are analysed, reviewed and discussed during the review section of the meeting. At the end of the academic year the rest of the columns are completed, analysed and discussed at the performance appraisal/review meeting with the team leader.

Action following the review

At the end of the review meeting a copy of the training and development needs for each team member is submitted to the personnel team leader. He/she creates a training and development action plan that is costed and forms a section of the school/business/improvement plan; this is later discussed with all staff and governors and, finally, ratified by the board of governors.

All action plans in the case study school follow the same or very similar format as the plans illustrated here, no matter if the plan relates to resources, staff development, personal targets or a building or curriculum development. The plans agreed for action and professional development are completed and attached to the cover sheet and the pupil progress sheets. In this way there is little prose writing and the documentation becomes a collection of action plans and pupil progress sheets easily completed at the time of target setting. The materials are not designed to be neat, tidy or attractive, but a collection of clear and agreed working targets and objectives.

These action plans inform the school's development plan, which is constructed around three areas: curriculum, personnel and resource, and finance. Each section of the plan is created, managed and monitored by a member of the leadership team, working with a team of governors and staff. In Figure 8.8 I give an example of two objectives from the personnel section of the development plan (strategic plan); note item 1 is to implement the 'individual training action plan' which is kept confidential to senior staff but costed and included in the development plan in this manner.

Links to professional development

In the case study school, professional development is linked almost totally to the needs identified in performance management. Training is consciously reduced in breadth but enhanced in terms of quality, impact and monitoring. For training and development to be regarded as effective it must impact on the individual member of staff, change a behaviour or process and be seen to impact on pupils and colleagues. The school's policy is offered below as a case study.

OBJECTIVE	LA EDP	HOW	SUCCESS CRITERIA	WHO	WHEN	COST £	DONE (date)
PERSONNEL:							
1. Implement individual training action plan.	1.3.a 1.4.a 1.4.c 1.5.b	As per plan.	As per plan.	BMS and team	March 04		
2. Continue to develop teachers' knowledge of 1CT and applications of 1CT skills.	1.2.a 1.2.b 1.3.a 1.3.b 1.3.c 1.6.a 1.6.a 1.6.d	• Personnel team to liaise with curriculum team to design training, development, classroom support • Coaching at QA meetings	• Training session deemed useful plus applied in the classroom • QA indicates application • Greater use observed during lesson obs	BMS team, PH, CMU.	June 03	£500	

Figure 8.8 *Example from the personnel section of a development plan*

TRAINING, DEVELOPMENT AND INDUCTION/MENTORING POLICY

The personnel section of the school Mission Statement states:

- ENCOURAGE EACH ADULT MEMBER OF THE SCHOOL TO REALISE HIS/HER POTENTIAL, REGARDLESS OF AGE, GENDER, RACE OR ABILITY.
- BE FORWARD LOOKING, POSITIVE AND FLEXIBLE ENOUGH TO RESPOND TO CHANGE.
- SUPPORT AND VALUE ALL MEMBERS OF THE SCHOOL AND ENSURE A WORK–LIFE BALANCE.

This indicates that the Senior Management Team, governors and all staff of Worth School are highly committed to, and greatly value, training and development. Worth School believes that receiving and providing high quality, effective training and development enables the organisation and individuals to continuously improve and develop. Well trained, well motivated and effective staff, governors and trainees are a valuable resource which can be used to provide a first class education for the pupils in our care.

TRAINING AND DEVELOPMENT PLAN

A Training and Development Plan is created by the Personnel Team Leader in consultation with the Senior Management Team, staff and governors. The plan contains training needs applicable to both individual members of staff and/or groups of staff. The plan identifies estimated course fees, cover and leave/costs. Generally needs identified are designed to improve the performance of an individual or group so as to improve the organisation's expertise and effectiveness. Training also takes place to equip individuals and groups to meet new requirements/policy or demands.

IDENTIFICATION

Individual needs are normally identified by the individual and their team leader through performance interviews. Group needs can be identified by performance interviews, staff/quality assurance meetings, assessment and review procedures which bring to light areas in need of development. Training is also used to equip individuals and groups to cope with changes in procedure and policy.

MANAGEMENT AND FUNDING OF TRAINING AND DEVELOPMENT

Training and development which is within policy and is not expensive is normally put into the Personnel Development Plan by the team leader after consultation with the personnel team. Courses which are not closely

(Continued)

linked to organisational needs or are expensive must be submitted to the whole governing body and staff moot for approval (for example long degree courses or secondments would need the express permission of the governing body).

PROCEDURES

Team:

- Once the Personnel Development Plan is set and agreed at the annual School Development Plan Moot, team meetings and training sessions are timetabled. All training and development is reviewed with regard to its effectiveness. In house training sessions are planned and reviewed upon completion. Courses, conferences or speakers are selected as appropriate. Review of external courses will also take place with further training planned if necessary.

Individual:

- Individual coaching, developments and training may be provided in house or externally. Individual staff or senior staff will select courses as per the Personnel Development Plan in consultation with the Personnel Team Leader.
- If an external course is booked the relevant course application forms and the pre-brief section of our course review sheet should be completed. These should be submitted to the Personnel Team Leader and signed. The course application should then be posted.
- Upon completion the review section of the form should be completed. The review should then be discussed with the Personnel Team Leader. The de-brief section should be completed and signed by the team leader. This should include costs. Further action should be agreed upon.
- The course advert and pre-brief form should be added to the individual's training and development file. The file will be reviewed during appraisal and part year to ensure targets are being met and results are forthcoming.

Governing Body:

- The procedure as stated above also applies to the governing body but governors do not have a formal appraisal made of their needs. Governors are requested to submit their training needs to the Head of Personnel, who will record needs. Governors will at times be 'encouraged' to attend training and development sessions as necessary.

(Continued)

(Continued)

AD HOC COURSES/CONFERENCES/BRIEFINGS

Occasionally coaching, development and courses need to be planned for individuals and groups to meet immediate and unforeseen needs. Such courses will be provided by the Head of Personnel if possible.

STAFF INDUCTION (For New and Internal Appointments/Transfers)

Senior staff and the school mentor ensure that the induction of new members of staff and new appointees is as smooth and effective as possible.

This policy and procedure has served the organisation well for many years. Whilst it values training and development, it also helps keep the process aligned with the needs of the organisation, stopping attendance at training and development events being random in nature.

Case study

In the case study school, kaizen led to the introduction of regular planning and preparation time for teachers and management time for team leaders, and this has been in place now for more than 15 years (which is not common in primary education in England). This time was introduced to enable team leaders and team members time to do the tasks required for performance coaching, training and development and management in quality time. Kaizen also brought about the inclusion of all support staff in the performance and professional development processes. Kaizen resulted in there being no weekly staff meetings and virtually all staff training and development being organised within work time, not in personal time. All training and development is carefully planned and focused into short and relevant sessions.

This ruthless focus on that which is needed saves precious time, goodwill and funds that are so often wasted in many organisations. Every event and development has an 'opportunity cost' and must be reviewed so that all resources are placed where and when they are most effective. The staff find it easy to review all important occurences and processes at the end of each event. It has become a habit to record what went well, what did not and to note suggestions relating to improvement. This is kaizen in action.

Return to the start of the performance cycle

It is at this point that the immediate action following the review meeting has been completed and the whole process starts again. This cycle of planning, action, monitoring and review is at the heart of the success of the case study school. The cycle ensures constant improvement and helps team members and team leaders focus on performance in a systematic yet manageable way.

Impact on your team?

I would suggest that this performance and motivation cycle has been the single most effective process introduced to the case study organisation. It promotes performance and motivation, and it is clear and professional. It helps align processes and attune vision and individual aspirations. I hope you found some use for this process in your work with your team.

Impact on you?

Now is the time to revisit the self-review you completed at the start of this chapter. Check if your team leaders and staff are ready for the appraisal meeting or not.

Before your next review meeting with one of your team will you have:	Yes	Partly	No
Agreed the date, venue and length of the meeting?			
Clearly established the focus and purpose of the meeting?			
Made sure all parties are clear about their roles and responsibilities?			
Agreed a venue that is comfortable and set out in an appropriate manner?			
Ensured all phone calls are diverted or taken by an answer machine?			

(Continued)

(Continued) Ensured a method of stopping others from entering the room or knocking on the door?			
Understood that this is a two-way process with both parties fully engaged?			
Agreed a school policy on confidentiality, who is to have access to any documentation and why?			
Agreed note-taking procedures and what will happen to the notes after the meeting?			
Analysed any target setting, self-review and monitoring materials?			
Ensured both parties are notified about any issues that might impact on the meeting?			
Agreed on a moderation process to ensure all involved have equal opportunity?			
Agreed who is to be sent copies of development objectives and agreed a recording format?			

These are the sort of practical matters that need a Yes answer. The attitude may be positive but the appraisal will go wrong if you are being interrupted, you are too hot, too cold or there is doubt as to the process and its purpose.

Repeat self-review

In the Introduction to this book I asked you to undertake two self-reviews. Now you have read the book, try these self-reviews again and see if you have made any progress.

Measuring the learning climate in your organisation		
There is little encouragement to learn new skills and abilities.	1 2 3 4 5	People are encouraged to extend themselves and their knowledge.
People are secretive; information is hoarded.	1 2 3 4 5	People share their views and information.

(Continued)		
People are ignored and then blamed when things go wrong.	1 2 3 4 5	People are recognised for good work and rewarded for learning.
People are not paid to think; their ideas are not valued.	1 2 3 4 5	Efforts are made to get people to share their ideas.
People do not help each other or share resources.	1 2 3 4 5	People are helpful, pleasure is taken in the success of others.
The higher you score, the more your organisation is likely to be a learning organisation.		

Now re-check your knowledge of the basics of performance management, as this is one of the key tools you can use in your drive to motivate your team's performance.

Performance coaching should be:	**Yes/Partly/No**
Integrated and inform training, development, target setting and development planning.	
A structured professional dialogue, based on objective progress/impact data, performance observations and appraisee self-review.	
Seen as being a key tool in helping teams focus on their core tasks.	
Transparent, rational, sustainable, low in bureaucracy and allows for unforeseen issues and problems that arise mid-year.	
Reviewed regularly by the users of the process with suggestions for improvement being accepted by senior staff, if feasible.	
Score: Yes = 2, Partly = 1, No = 0. **The fewer points scored out of 10, the more you need to update your knowledge of effective performance management.**	

How did you do this second time? If you still have gaps in your knowledge read some of the works listed in 'Further reading'.

Further reading

Adair, J. (1982) *Effective Time Management*. London: Pan.

Department for Education and Employment (DfEE) (2001) *Good Value CPD*. DfEE 0059/2001. London: The Stationery Office.

Early, P. and Bubb, S. (2004) *Leading and Managing Continuing Professional Development*. London: Paul Chapman Publishing.

Gardener, H. Kornhaber, M. and Wake, W. (1996) *Intelligence: Multiple Perspective*. London: Harcourt Brace.

Goleman, D. (1995) *Emotional Intelligence*. London: Bartam.

Goleman, D. (1998) *Working with Emotional Intelligence*. London: Bloomsbury.

Reading, M. and Smith, A. (2003) 'The implications of performance management in the UK', conference paper for the International Congress for School Effectiveness and Improvement, 19 December, 2002, Sydney.

Bibliography

Adair, J. (1982) *Effective Time Management*. London: Pan.

Argyris, C. (1978) 'A leadership dilemma: skilled incompetence', in C. Argyris and D. Schon, *Organisational Learning: A Theory of Action Perspective*. London: Addison-Wesley.

Argyris, C. (1999) *On Organizational Learning*. 2nd edn. Oxford: Blackwell.

Argyris, C. and Schon, D. (1974) *Theory in Practice: Increasing Professional Effectiveness*. San Francisco, CA: Jossey Bass.

Block, P. (2000) *Flawless Consultancy: A Guide to Getting Your Expertise Used*. 2nd edn. San Francisco, CA: Jossey Bass.

Boyatzis, R. (1999) 'Self-directed change and learning as a necessary meta-competency for success and effectiveness in the twenty-first century', in R. Sims and J. Veres (eds), *Keys to Employee Success in Coming Decades*. Westport, CT: Quorum Books.

Brighouse, T. and Woods, D. (1999) *How to Improve Your School*. London: Routledge.

Byham, C. and Cox, J. (1998) *Zapp: The Lightning of Empowerment*. London: Century Business.

Caldwell, B. and Spinks, J. (1992) *Leading the Self Managing School*. London: Falmer Press.

Carnell, E. (2006) 'Mentoring, coaching and learning: examining the connections', *Professional Development Today*, spring.

Catholic Education Service (2000) *Performance Management in Catholic Schools*. Nottingham: Midland Regional Printers.

Cheshire Advisory Service (n.d.) *A Handbook: School Teacher Appraisal*. Chester: Cheshire County Council.

Cockman, P., Evans, B. and Reynolds, P. (1999) *Consulting for Real People*. Maidenhead: McGraw-Hill.

Collins, J. (2001) *From Good to Great*. London: Random House Business Books.

Cordingley, P. (2006) 'Coaching and mentoring: a national framework?', *Professional Development Today*, spring.

Covey, S. (1989) *The Seven Habits of Highly Effective People*. New York: Simon and Schuster.

Creasy, J. and Paterson, F. (2005) *Leading Coaching in Schools*. Nottingham: National College for School Leadership.

Department for Education and Employment (DfEE) (1991) *Education (School Teacher Appraisal) Regulations 1991*. London: The Stationery Office.

Department for Education and Employment (DfEE) (2000a) *Performance Management in Schools: Model Performance Management Policy*. London: The Stationery Office.

Department for Education and Employment (DfEE) (2000b) *Performance Management in Schools: Performance Management Framework*. DfEE 0051/2000. London: The Stationery Office.

Department for Education and Employment (DfEE) (2000c) *Performance Management Toolkit for PMCs*. London: The Stationery Office.

Department for Education and Employment (DfEE) (2001) *Good Value CPD*. DfEE 0059/2001. London: The Stationery Office.

Department for Education and Employment (DfEE) (n.d.) *Getting the Most From Your Data*. London: Standards and Effectiveness Unit.

Department for Education and Skills (DfES) (2002) *Embedding Performance Management: Training Modules*. London: DfES.

Department for Education and Skills (DfES) (2006) *The Education (School Teacher Performance Management) (England) Regulations 2006*. London: DfES.

Drucker, P. (1986) *The Frontiers of Management*. London: Heinemann.

Early, P. and Bubb, S. (2004) *Leading and Managing Continuing Professional Development*. London: Paul Chapman Publishing.

Egan, G. (1993) *Adding Value: A Systematic Guide to Business Driven Management and Leadership*. San Francisco, CA: Jossey-Bass.

Egan, G. (1998) *The Skilled Helper: A Problem-Management and Opportunity-Development Approach to Helping*. 6th edn. London and Pacific Grove, CA: Brooks/Cole.

Esp, D. and Saran, R. (1995) *Effective Governors for Effective Schools*. London: Pitman.

Evans, R. (1998) *The Human Side of School Change*. San Francisco, CA: Jossey-Bass.

Fullan, M. (1991) *The New Meaning of Educational Change*. London: Cassell.

Fullan, M. (1993) *Change Forces*. London: Falmer Press.

Gann, N. (1999) *Targets for Tomorrow's Schools*. London: Falmer Press.

Gardener, H., Kornhaber, M. and Wake, W. (1996) *Intelligence: Multiple Perspectives*. London: Harcourt Brace.

Garret, B. (1990) *Creating a Learning Organisation*. Hemel Hempstead: Director Books, Fitzwilliam.

Gold, A., Evans, J., Early, P., Halpin, D. and Collarbone, P. (2003) 'Principled principals?', *Educational Management and Administration*, 31(2): 127–38.

Goleman, D. (1995) *Emotional Intelligence*. London: Bantam.

Goleman, D. (1998) *Working with Emotional Intelligence*. London: Bloomsbury.

Goleman, D. (2003) *Destructive Emotions and How We Can Overcome Them*. London: Bloomsbury.

Hammer, M. and Champy, J. (1994) *Reengineering the Corporation*. London: Nicholas Brealey.

Handy, C. (1989) *The Age of Unreason*. London: Arrow Business Books.

Hargreaves, D. and Hopkins, D. (1991) *The Empowered School*. London: Cassell.

Hartle, F. (1999) 'Performance management in schools: moving out of the tick box', speech to BEMAS/Industrial Society, London.

Heron, J. (1999) *The Complete Facilitator's Handbook*. London and New York: Kogan Page.

Johnson, J. (1998) *Who Moved My Cheeses?* New York: G.P. Putnam's Sons.

Jones, J. (2006) 'Coaching for better staff performance', *Professional Development Today*, spring.

Joy, B. (2006) 'Trained mentor-coaches – making a difference', *Professional Development Today*, spring.

Lawson, I. (1999) *Leaders for Tomorrow's Society*. London: The Industrial Society.

McGrane, J. (2006) 'Does coaching make a difference?', *Professional Development Today*, spring.

Miliband, D. (2003) 'School improvement and performance management', speech to the Performance Management Conference, Bournemouth. Available at info@dfes.gsi.gov.uk.

Mintzberg, H. (1973) *The Nature of Managerial Work*. New York: HarperCollins.

Mortimer, P., Sammons, P., Stoll, L. Lewis, D. and Ecob, R. (1998) *School Matters*. Wells: Open Books.

Nonaka, I. and Takeuchi, H. (1995) *The Knowledge Creating Company: How Japanese Companies Create the Dynamic of Innovation*. New York: Oxford University Press.

Ofsted (2006) Ofsted inspection report, January 2006 for Worth Primary School. Ofsted. www.ofsted.gov.uk, page 2.

Osterman, K. and Kottkamp, R. (1994) 'Rethinking professional development', in N. Bennett, R. Glatter and R. Levacic (eds), *Improving Educational Management*. London: Paul Chapman Publishing.

Parkin, M. (2001) *Coaching and Storytelling*. London: Kogan Page.

Pedler, M., Burgoyne, J. and Boydell, T. (1991) *The Learning Company: A Strategy for Sustainable Development*. Maidenhead: McGraw-Hill.

Peters, T. and Waterman, R. (1982) *In Search of Excellence*. New York and London: Harper and Row.

Reading, M. (2003) 'Still on the cycle', *Management in Education*, 16(5).

Reading, M. and Smith, A. (2003) 'The implications of performance management in the UK', conference paper for the International Congress for School Effectiveness and Improvement, Sydney.

Rowan, J. and Taylor, P. (2002) 'Leading the autonomous school', in J. Heywood and P. Taylor (eds), *School Autonomy*. European Forum on Educational Administration, Bulletin 2.

Rutter, M., Maughan, B., Mortimore, B and Quston, J. (1979) *Fifteen Thousand Hours: Secondary Schools and Their Effects on Children*. London: Open Books.

Schein, E. (1984) 'Coming to a new awareness of organizational culture', *Sloan Management Review*, 25(2): 3–16.

Schein, E.H. (1999) *Process Consultation Revisited*. Reading, MA: Addison-Wesley.

Senge, P. (1990) *The Fifth Discipline*. London: Nicholas Brealey.

Senge, P., Lucas, T. and Dutton, J. (2000) *Schools that Learn*. London: Nicholas Brealey.

Senge, P.M. (1990) *The Fifth Discipline: The Age and Practice of the Learning Organisation*. London: Century Press.

Southworth, G. and Conner, C. (1999) *Managing Improving Primary Schools*. London: Falmer Press.

Tabberer, R., Hine, T. and Gallagher, S. (1996) 'Seven obstacles to effective target setting', *Education Journal*, 7.

Wellins, R., Byham, W. and Wilson, J. (1991) *Empowered Teams*. San Francisco, CA: Jossey-Bass.

Index